WRITERS AND THEIR WORK

ISOBEL ARMSTRONG
General Editor

BRYAN LOUGHREY
Advisory Editor

MEASURE FOR MEASURE

Dan Meaden as Mistress Overdone in the 1974 RSC production of *Measure for Measure* directed by Keith Hack.

William Shakespeare

MEASURE FOR MEASURE

KATE CHEDGZOY

Northcote House
in association with the
British Council

First published in 2000 by Northcote House Publishers Ltd, Horndon House,
Horndon, Tavistock, Devon, PL19 9NQ, United Kingdom.
Tel: +44 (01822) 810066 Fax: +44 (01822) 810034.

British Library Cataloguing-in-Publication Data
A catalogue record for this book is available from the British Library

ISBN 0-7463-0849-3

Typeset by PDQ Typesetting, Newcastle-under-Lyme
Printed and bound in Great Britain by
The Baskerville Press, Salisbury, Wiltshire, SP2 7QB

Contents

Acknowledgements

I am grateful to the series editors: Brian Loughrey for giving me the opportunity to write on *Measure for Measure*, and Isobel Armstrong for her attentive and thoughtful response to my drafts. Thanks are due to the Shakespeare Centre Library, Stratford-upon-Avon, and to Cheek by Jowl theatre company, for permission to consult and use production archives, and to the Birmingham Shakespeare Library for generous assistance with illustrations.

With her customary intellectual acuity and generosity, Julie Sanders helped me find a way into *Measure for Measure*, and then, as an interlocutor in many real and imagined conversations, enabled me to go on writing about it. Clare McManus rendered measure for measure, but was merciful. The book was mainly written in the Cottage Street House of Correction Studies, where Di Paton was an exacting and inspiring cell-mate; she has taught me a great deal about love and justice. Many other friends and colleagues shared ideas and offered encouragement, and I am grateful to them all.

References

All references to *Measure for Measure* and other Shakespearian texts are to the Oxford *William Shakespeare: The Complete Works*, general editors Stanley Wells and Gary Taylor (Oxford: Clarendon Press, 1988).

Illustrations

Introduction

Almost four centuries after its first performance, 1994 was the year of *Measure for Measure*. In Britain, two major theatre companies, the Royal Shakespeare Company, whose privileged cultural status is indicated by its name, and the more alternative, adventurous Cheek by Jowl, both staged major productions, while a third version of the play was filmed and broadcast by the BBC. This surge of interest in Shakespeare's play proved timely. Although the productions must all have been planned long before, they actually reached the public domain at a moment when the Conservative government in Britain was attempting – with, as it turned out, little success – to increase its popularity by means of the so-called back-to-basics campaign, involving a new focus on personal morality, defined essentially as sexual morality, as the foundation of social order. In modern politics and in *Measure for Measure* alike, the sexual is made into the touchstone of morality by the forces of secular power. Through the events that unfold in this play, Shakespeare exposes the problems and complications that attend the interaction of politics and sexuality on the social stage.

Reviewers of these 1994 productions repeatedly pointed out the extraordinary relevance of the play to the contemporary political scene. Some even went so far as to offer interpretations of the play as a kind of prophetic allegory, suggesting which members of the government might most appropriately play the central roles. But these issues are not merely of domestic, British interest. By a richly suggestive coincidence, it was also in late October 1994, just as the Royal Shakespeare Company's *Measure for Measure* was opening at Stratford-upon-Avon and the BBC was screening David Thacker's production, that on the other side of the Atlantic a previously obscure young woman called Paula Jones was first bringing charges of sexual harassment

1

against US President Bill Clinton. It doesn't seem quite right to claim Paula Jones as an Isabella for our times. Nevertheless, her accusations vividly demonstrate the complex intertwining of sex and power, and among their repercussions was an international public debate about precisely those questions of truth and testimony, justice and authority, religion and politics that are explored in *Measure for Measure*.

The contemporary echoes of *Measure for Measure* are audible far beyond Britain and the USA. On his return to England after touring the world with Cheek by Jowl's production, director Declan Donnellan remarked in an interview on BBC Radio 4, 'In different countries on this long tour they've all said it's absolutely amazing, how brilliant of you to choose to bring *Measure for Measure* of all plays to our country because it's so topical because our government is wracked with corruption scandals at the moment. We go from Tokyo to Perth...to Brazil...to Buenos Aires.' Donnellan went on to suggest that the play's apparently global relevance could be explained by the fact that 'where you have government you tend also to have some kind of abuse of it'.[1]

At the end of the twentieth century, a time exceptionally preoccupied with the relations between the personal and the political, private morality and public behaviour, sexuality and power, *Measure for Measure* achieved a relevance to current affairs unparalleled since it was first staged in 1604. This can be seen as the culmination of a century-long process that has made the play into one that speaks very directly and challengingly – though with many different voices – to the modern age. Looking back from 1972 over the fortunes of Shakespeare's problem plays in the preceding half-century, Michael Jamieson argued that they had 'undergone a revaluation so radical as to amount to a rediscovery, and this reassessment itself reflects changes in literary and historical taste'.[2] This process has, if anything, accelerated in the subsequent quarter century. Later in this study, I will sketch an account of *Measure for Measure*'s history, on stage and in culture, showing how it has gone from being relatively little performed and little discussed to occupying a position among the most frequently staged and written about of Shakespeare's plays.

In Freud's century, it is hardly surprising that *Measure for*

Measure's intense exploration of sexuality and its place in society has fascinated audiences and critics. But the play's engagement with questions of ethics and politics as they bear on all aspects of social existence is also of compelling interest and relevance. In 1836, Richard Wagner's opera *Das Liebesverbot* (*The Ban on Love*) took *Measure for Measure* as its starting point and politicized the play's basic situation in a way characteristic of that age of movements for national liberation and revolution: at the close of the opera, Isabella becomes a revolutionary heroine, rousing the oppressed masses to rebel against the viceroy (Angelo's counterpart) and free Claudio. Almost a century later, one of the most influential modern exponents of the political Shakespeare, Bertolt Brecht, also drew on *Measure for Measure* as the inspiration for a play that engaged directly with some of the most pressing political and ethical concerns of the 1930s, *The Round-Heads and the Pointy-Heads*. Brecht's original purpose was to write a play that offered a Marxist account of the corruption of law and justice by the rich and powerful. It is not hard to see why *Measure for Measure*, which he always considered the most radical of Shakespeare's plays, seemed to provide fertile material for adaptation. However, as the play was reworked over a period from about 1931 to 1936, the growing dominance of the Nazi party, and the increasingly murderous character of their anti-Semitic policies, promoted him to draw issues of racial intolerance into the scope of the drama. The play is set in the state of Yahoo, home to two different ethnic groups: the round-heads and the pointy-heads of the title. The rich (but racially inferior) pointy-head Guzman is sentenced to death, ostensibly for a sexual assault on a round-head woman, though in fact property interests underlie the accusation. The Hitler-like deputy Angelo is willing to spare Guzman if his beautiful sister Isabella will go to bed with him. As in Shakespeare's play, the substitution of one woman for another enables the heroine to maintain her chastity, but Brecht presses on the contradictory sexual politics of *Measure for Measure* by making the stand-in a prostitute, whose profiteering madam nominates her for the task.

Though it differs substantially from Shakespeare's original, Brecht's play does not so much impose wholly new meanings on *Measure for Measure* as bring into prominence concerns that are marginal or latent there. As he revised it with an eye to the

3

rise of Fascism in Europe, *The Round-Heads and the Pointy-Heads* became a play in which the theme of class conflict intertwined with a comical, satirical attack on racism and anti-semitism. Though *Measure for Measure* seems to offer less promising material for considering the representation of racial or cultural difference than some of Shakespeare's other plays, such as *Antony and Cleopatra* or *The Tempest*, Brecht's appropriation of the play to deal with these issues has, intriguingly, been echoed in recent productions that have employed cross-racial casting or post-colonial settings. At the National Theatre in London, for instance, a 1981 production employing a cast of black actors, many of them of Caribbean descent, located *Measure for Measure* on a Caribbean island trying to work out the principles that should underlie its self-government after centuries of colonial domination. Critical reactions at the time demonstrated all too clearly that many reviewers still preferred to think of the world of Shakespeare's play as an entirely white one, but such productions open up the possibility of understanding the dramatic uses of racial and cultural difference in more complex and sophisticated ways. Fostered by noteworthy productions like this one, as well as by the work of black-led companies such as Tara Arts and Talawa, the practice of integrated casting – choosing performers because they will handle a role well, regardless of ethnicity or physical appearance – has gained ground in the British theatre over the 1980s and 1990s. So by the time Cheek by Jowl cast black performers Danny Sapani as Claudio, and Marianne Jean-Baptiste in an imaginative doubling of the roles of Mariana and Mrs Overdone, it was their acting, and not their ethnicity, that was considered worthy of comment: both performers were widely acclaimed. The exploration of racial and cultural difference has been an important and productive development in recent Shakespearian criticism. In the case of *Measure for Measure*, it might seem that such a project is restricted to pointing out the exclusion of difference and the unexamined centrality of whiteness. Performance shows that this need not be the case, although openness to the new possibilities represented by difference brings its own challenges.

What is missing from this brief preliminary sketch of some of the main concerns of *Measure for Measure* is religion. To leave it aside in this way would undoubtedly have seemed bizarre and inexplicable to members of the original audience for the play, inhabitants of a society where everyday life was saturated with religious beliefs, practices, and controversies. And indeed Christian concepts are central to the play. Its title is drawn directly from the New Testament, from the section of Matthew's Gospel known as the Sermon on the Mount, which is often seen as summing up Christianity's essential prescriptions concerning personal morality. To place the phrase in context: 'Judge not, that you be not judged. For with the judgement you pronounce you will be judged, and the measure you give will be the measure you get' (Matt. 7: 1–2). This is essentially the argument that Isabella uses to Angelo when, with what will later prove to be crushing irony, she advises him to scrutinize his own behaviour, and to consider whether he is really in a position to pass judgement on Claudio:

> Go to your bosom,
> Knock there, and ask your heart what it doth know
> That's like my brother's fault; if it confess
> A natural guiltiness, such as is his,
> Let it not sound a thought upon your tongue
> Against my brother's life.

> (2.2.140–5)

It is an approach to justice that counsels mercy, self-awareness, and a sense of the reciprocal bonds that hold society together. The moral demand to imagine oneself in another person's situation is embodied in the play by the series of substitutions that carry the plot forward: Angelo for the Duke, Mariana for Isabella, Ragosine's head for Claudio's. Many people have felt that advocacy of this New Testament ethic is *Measure for Measure*'s ultimate message.

But there is also another way of interpreting the title in the light of biblical precepts – one that is given weight by the play's only use of the biblical phrase that provides its title, in the Duke's insistence in the final scene on retributive justice:

> 'An Angelo for Claudio, death for death'.
> Haste still pays haste, and leisure answers leisure;
> Like doth quit like, and measure still for measure.

> (5.1.406–8)

5

What the Duke invokes here is the principle of talion justice, in which the punishment is supposed to fit the crime; in the terms of the Old Testament, an eye for an eye, a tooth for a tooth. Bloodthirsty though this sounds, we should recall that it was designed to limit the scale of retribution: no more than an eye should be taken in revenge for an eye. But it obviously represents a more vengeful and punitive attitude than the Sermon on the Mount, one which Isabella – and arguably, with her the play – ultimately rejects when she joins Mariana in pleading for mercy. Even Lucio's punishment is partially remitted, despite the Duke's hostility towards him. Yet, though mercy provides the play with its comic closure, *Measure for Measure* opens up no dramatic space in which to explore the question of how such an approach to justice might work in social practice.

Measure for Measure ultimately opts for the principles embedded in the Christian Sermon on the Mount, rather than the Old Testament principle of talion justice common to the other religions of the book. In the mid-twentieth century, a number of literary critics sought to emphasize this Christian aspect to the play, and to interpret it allegorically, although they fell some way short of achieving consensus concerning the precise allegorical significance of the play. One influential example, G. Wilson Knight's essay '*Measure for Measure* and the Gospels', presents the play as a moral drama in which the central characters embody Christian figures or concepts. Lucio's name is the warrant for casting him as the demonic Lucifer. In contrast, the Duke is perceived entirely positively: 'The Duke's sense of human responsibility is delightful throughout: he is like a kindly father, and all the rest are his children'; he is 'the prophet of a new order of ethics' who 'tends to assume proportions evidently divine'.[3] It is hard to imagine anyone now producing such a positive and enthusiastic account: modern scholarship and stagings more often side with Lucio's description of 'the old fantastical Duke of dark corners' (4.3.152–3).

Even if this way of interpreting the play may now seem to be of limited use, it is clear that Christian beliefs and ways of making sense of the world underpin its moral structure, as well as providing a framework for the social world in which the events take place: a world inhabited by friars, puritans, and nuns-to-be. It would be misleading to suggest that this Christian ethos and atmosphere would have been taken for granted in Shakespeare's England. Far from it: throughout the preceding century, Christian doctrine and practice had been matters of fierce controversy, leading to state-sponsored violence and bloody resistance all across Europe. Nevertheless, within the European world view to which Shakespeare was subject, the centrality of Christianity as the dominant religion remained unexamined. Now, though, we must make sense of the specifically Christian elements of *Measure for Measure* in a world marked by the opposing tides of secularism and fundamentalism, where in some regions Christianity's taken-for-granted centrality has been displaced by multiculturalism, in others it has never been the dominant religion or a major social force, and in yet others it has emerged as a vital social, spiritual, and political power. In the face of the ethical, moral, and political volatility that we all now live with, it is no surprise that *Measure for Measure*, this strange and complex play, continually accrues new significance and new resonance in the modern world.

1

Our City's Institutions

In the first scene of *Measure for Measure*, the Duke's opening speech foregrounds concepts crucial to the play: 'government' (1.1.3.), 'the nature of our people' (1.1.10), 'Our city's institutions, and the terms/For common justice' (1.1.10–11). As he compliments Escalus on his wisdom and competence in matters relating to the government of Vienna, he gestures towards these key political concepts in a manner that assumes that he and Escalus – and, implicitly, the audience too – share a common understanding and evaluation of what they mean. But this is precisely what the events of the play will call into question. In this chapter, I examine Shakespeare's depiction of those institutions that are most closely associated with the exercise of power and the maintenance of social order in Vienna; the Ducal court, the court of law, and the prison.

Modern editions of *Measure for Measure* are all based on the text printed in the First Folio, the collected volume published in 1623 that forms the basis of the Shakespeare canon. Editors often choose to open the play with a stage direction – in the Oxford edition I am using, 'Enter Duke, Escalus, and other Lords', implying a formal, ceremonial entrance in which the Duke is attended by numbers of courtiers. However, the First Folio text has very few stage directions, and simply launches straight into the exchange between the Duke and Escalus. At least one attendant needs to be present in order to go and summon Angelo on the duke's instruction at line 15: but need it be assumed that he is part of a substantial courtly retinue? The question of whether this opening scene involves a low-key transaction of business in the Duke's private closet, or a public ceremonial for the ostentatious handover of power, is not just relevant to deciding how the scene should be staged, but has

Fig. 1. Title page of *Measure for Measure,* in Cassell's Illustrated Shakespeare (1865): a Victorian vision of a distinctly Gothic Vienna.

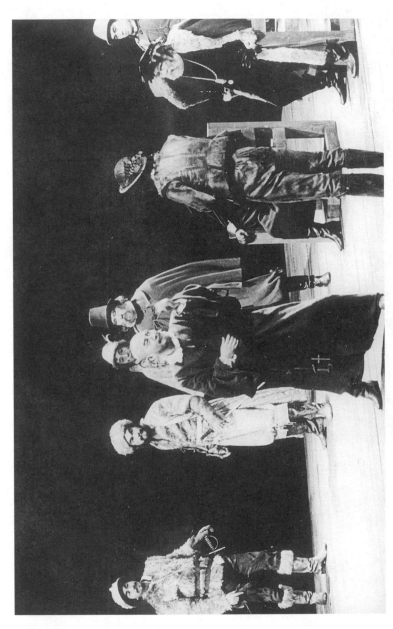

Fig. 2. A production of *Measure for Measure* at the Peking People's Arts Theatre, 1981, illustrating the global reach of the play at the end of the twentieth century.

implications for the whole question of how power is exercised in Vienna. The idea that monarchy and the exercise of royal authority in this period were theatrical and spectacular by nature has been widely discussed, drawing support from two comments on this subject made by Elizabeth I and James VI and I.[1] Addressing a deputation from Parliament in 1586, Elizabeth reportedly remarked, 'We princes are set upon stages in the sight and view of all the world' ('princes' here is a gender-neutral term, meaning simply 'rulers').[2] At first sight, this seems to be a declaration of the political power that resided in her uniquely spectacular position. But it can arguably be seen as a sign of her anxiety and vulnerability: the deputation was asking her to sign the death warrant of Mary Queen of Scots, and she must have wondered what the consequences of this would be, and what the world would make of her actions.

A few decades later, James (son of Mary Queen of Scots) wrote *Basilicon Doron*, a treatise on kingship in which he warned his own son that a ruler should limit and control his public appearances, noting that 'a King is as one set on a scaffold, whose smallest actions and gestures all the people gazingly do behold'.[3] The word 'scaffold' at this time referred both to the theatrical stage and to the platform where executions were carried out, and so this formulation emphasizes more strongly than Elizabeth's the vulnerability that goes with being the object of so many gazes. Perhaps with this in mind, in later editions of *Basilicon Doron* James emended the dangerously ambiguous term 'scaffold' to 'stage'.

Towards the end of the first scene, the Duke's claim that 'I love the people, / But do not like to stage me to their eyes' (1.1.68–9) signals a preference for a discreet, modest employment of his authority – although this is not wholly borne out by the gusto with which he sustains his disguise as Friar Lodowick, and manipulates the elaborate stagings of the final scene. Scholars have likened the Duke's attitude here to King James's reticent self-presentation and alleged distaste for crowds. When *Measure for Measure* was written, James had only very recently come to the throne of England and Wales, and throughout the early months of his reign the danger of plague had the effect of curtailing all aspects of public life, so that he must have initially seemed to be a surprisingly self-effacing ruler. Accounts of

9

Measure for Measure that seek to understand the play within its historical context often see it as a Jacobean play, relating its treatment of governance and the ruler to James himself. But it should be remembered that the play was written and performed very early in James's reign, a period that might more usefully be understood as one of change and transition after the long reign of Elizabeth I rather than in terms of the imposition of a full-blown Jacobean regime. Recognizing this, some critics have seen *Measure for Measure* as an example of a sub-genre of 'disguised-ruler' plays that had a brief vogue in the early part of James's reign, and that were clearly concerned with making sense of the change of regime. Frank Whigham describes the characteristics of this genre as follows:

> a superior figure absents himself from court, disguising himself as a subject and producing a climate of surveillance; from this vantage he observes and comments upon others' privy desires, political, social and sexual; these devices are amplified by the opportunity-vacuum his absence creates; he encourages their indulgence, exposes the actors to public justice, and reaps and purveys various benefits, personal as well as collective.[4]

Central to the 'disguised-ruler' genre is the choosing and testing of the substitute who is to deputize for the king or duke in his absence. It is a form that sees power as lying in the hands of the individual at the head of the court, rather than in the court itself as a collective force. The Duke will maintain control in his absence by using Angelo and Escalus as tools or instruments – 'we have...given his deputation all the organs/Of our own power' (1.1.17, 21–2) – a notion that finds an ironically apt echo in the claim, made by Angelo himself in the final scene, that Isabella and Mariana are 'instruments of some more mightier member/That sets them on' (5.1.235–6). It is often suggested that, in this role as orchestrator of the events that unfold in Vienna, the Duke is reminiscent of a playwright or stage manager. As Jonathan Goldberg puts it, 'In the Duke, Shakespeare has written a role that represents his powers as a playwright as coincident with the powers of the sovereign.'[5] The Duke who wields such all-embracing control over Vienna prefigures another Duke who has often been seen as a figure for Shakespeare himself: Prospero, who deploys theatrical magic to sustain his rule over his island domain in *The Tempest*.

The idea that Angelo is to be a substitute for the Duke is emphasized by the Duke's query, 'What figure of us think you he will bear?' (1.1.16). This is the first of the play's numerous references to the stamping of an impression on a surface, as with a coin, seal, or printing press, and it is soon echoed in Angelo's reluctance to accept the Duke's commission:

> Now, good my lord,
> Let there be some more test made of my mettle,
> Before so noble and so great a figure
> Be stamped upon it.

(1.1.47–50)

The image recurs throughout the play, a symptom of its central concern with the outward legibility of people's inward nature. The Duke's query 'What figure of us think you he will bear?' draws the nexus of images of stamping, character, and so on together with concerns about substitution, performance, and impersonation. His remark a few lines later, 'Angelo,/There is a kind of character in thy life/That to the observer doth thy history/Fully unfold' (1.1.26–9), develops this theme in a way that comes to bear a retrospective irony, as the events of the play unfold a mismatch between Angelo's virtuous public appearance and his private behaviour. In *Measure for Measure* the word 'character' is most often used to imply that outward appearance can be taken as a transparent indicator of personal history; but it is also worth recalling the notion of 'character' as a cipher for secret communication. As in other plays, such as *Romeo and Juliet* or *King Lear*, there is an important connection in *Measure for Measure* between the employment of deputies, the exchange of messages, and the maintenance of disguise or secrecy; and all too often, it seems, Shakespearian delegates, like Angelo, exceed, betray, or prove untrustworthy in their commissions.

If the Duke's court is the primary institution of the Viennese city state, the prison, where the legal policies authorized by the ducal court are put into effect, is also a crucial site of power. The longest scene of *Measure for Measure*, which is also at its centre, occupying the whole of Act 3 in the Oxford edition I am using, takes place in prison. At some point in the play virtually everyone is found to be residing in or passing through Vienna's

11

prison, so that the boundaries that separate the world outside
the prison walls and the world within them dissolve. In another
play, Hamlet complains that 'Denmark's a prison' (*Hamlet*,
2.2.246), and here it seems that the same could almost be said of
Vienna. Jacques Lezra finds that the world of the play consists of
two distinct social realms, functioning as a kind of mirror of each
other, the court of Vienna and the prison: 'Both have distinct
political hierarchies ranged under single rulers with analogous
deputizing powers who share a taste for the theatrical
manipulation of their subjects.'[6] Lezra suggests that the
processes by which the Duke seeks to achieve social order in
Vienna and to reform his wayward subjects' behaviour are
equivalent to the means that the Provost uses to control and
reform the inmates of his prison. Specifically, we could liken the
Duke's instruction to Claudio to reconcile himself to the
inevitability of execution and cultivate a spirit of resignation
that allows him to 'Be absolute for death' (3.1.5–41) to the
Provost's repeated attempts to stimulate an equally suitable
attitude to death in the recalcitrant criminal, Barnardine: 'We
have very oft awaked him, as if to carry him to execution, and
showed him a seeming warrant for it; it hath not moved him at
all' (4.2.150–2). Barnadine's zest for continued life, however
squalid, and stalwart resistance to this moral manipulation make
him an engaging character who marks the limits of the law's
ability to compel a particular response from its subjects.

This equivalence between the city at large and the prison
creates a powerful and unsettling image of civic life, suggesting
the extent to which all the citizens of Vienna are constantly
subject to surveillance and discipline, however free they may
believe themselves to be. Relevant here is the dual meaning of
the word 'court', as a place where alleged criminals are tried and
punished or freed, but also – under a monarchial or ducal
political regime – as the seat of the power that underlies the
legal system. The script of *Measure for Measure* rarely identifies
particular locations, but some editors have identified particular
scenes as taking place in a court in either of these senses: Act 2,
Scene 1, for example, has all the characteristics of a courtroom
scene, whether or not it is literally set in one. It is arguable that
whether or not this scene takes place in an actual courtroom is
beside the point, because what happens in this play is that

Vienna itself becomes a place where people are put on trial. And, like the 'court', 'trial' here has a dual meaning, referring both to a forced encounter with the legal system, and to the notion of being put to the test, made to undergo an ordeal. Thus, in the culmination of a process that structures the whole play, the final scene makes the public space of the city itself into a kind of courtroom, a place where people are brought to trial, judgment is passed, and justice done. For example, the capacity of Escalus and Angelo to dispense justice is assessed, vindicated in the one instance, and revealed to be entirely fraudulent in the other – even though Angelo so insistently demands to be put to the test, secure in his sense of his own virtue at the beginning of the play, in a way that will not survive the more demanding trial of his encounter with Isabella. Isabella in turn undergoes her own test when Mariana begs her to join in pleading for the life of the man who assaulted the chastity on which she places such a high value, and was also, as she believes, responsible for the dubiously legal execution of her beloved brother.

The ideas about law and power outlined above are informed by the work of the French thinker Michel Foucault, whose book on the history of European penal systems, *Discipline and Punish*, has had a considerable influence on Shakespeare criticism in the last decade or so. Richard Wilson, one of the most forceful exponents of a Foucauldian approach to Shakespeare, has recently offered both an account and a demonstration of this critical practice with particular reference to *Measure for Measure*. He suggests that there is a special kind of relationship between Foucault and Shakespeare because the latter was an acute observer of what Foucault calls 'the Great Confinement': the establishment of those institutions of surveillance and discipline that were to be fundamental to the structuring of modern societies. Surveillance is central to Foucault's work, where it describes the process by which people's behaviour is controlled by their sense that they are continually watched over by an authority figure who is not reciprocally subject to their scrutiny. This is clearly relevant to the Duke's decision to restore order in his city by means of apparent absence and secretive manipulation, facilitated by the disguise that allows him to spy on his subjects, and to insert himself into their confidence by encouraging them to confess their fears, desires, and anxieties to him. In an influential discussion of the disciplinary uses of surveillance in *Measure for Measure*, Jonathan Dollimore invokes the Renaissance debate concerning the Machiavellian understanding of religion as a means of ideological and social control, which worked by inciting people to discipline themselves, to internalize their own submission.[7] This is what is at stake when the Duke tries to encourage Claudio to accept the judgment of Church and State and 'Be absolute for death' (3.1.5–41), and in the Provost's attempts to make Barnardine accept his status as a condemned criminal (4.2.150–2). Thus the Duke's adoption of religious disguise does not merely have the theatrical advantage of providing him with a costume that includes a face-concealing hood, but also allows him to appropriate the Church's capacity for social control. Richard Wilson argues that the Duke's particular choice of the role of travelling Friar for his disguise can be understood in terms of Foucault's account of 'the historical process whereby modern secular institutions, such as hospitals and prisons, appropriated the language, confessionals, and often the very buildings, of medieval religious orders: a process which seems to be personified by the Duke when he dresses as a monk.'[8] It is a pleasing irony that one of the novel institutions of Shakespeare's London that had carried out such an appropriation was the theatre. More than one of the private, indoor theatres was accommodated in what had, prior to Henry VIII's seizure of Church property, been a religious house: one example, as its name indicates, is Blackfriars, on which Shakespeare's own company, the King's Men, had a lease. The theatre does, of course, play a very different social role from the institutions named by Wilson, and the precise nature of the dynamic relation between theatrical performance and social practice remained controversial and contested throughout Shakespeare's career. Though some playwrights argued for the beneficial effects of drama, claiming that it offered opportunities to set models of desirable behaviour before audiences and thereby inculcate socially responsible attitudes, it was often perceived as a place of potential disorder, if not actual crime and sedition.

Another distinctly Foucauldian institution that, in Shakespeare's time, occupied former Church property was the Bridewell, London's principal house of correction. Conventionally, penal policy – especially the kind of which imprisonment is a central plank – has four main aims: incapacitation, deterrence, retribution, and reformation. How do the punishments used and threatened in *Measure for Measure* answer to this range of requirements? Implicitly or explicitly, all four are called on by the Viennese penal system. Perhaps predictably, incapacitation, which offers rather limited dramatic possibilities, is the least significant – indeed, the somewhat chaotic nature of the prison regime seems to offer opportunities to engage in a life of crime even while incarcerated. The Duke's important speech in which he explains to Friar Thomas his motives for leaving the government of Vienna – appointing Angelo as his deputy with the task of unleashing 'tied-up justice', and adopting disguise to monitor the outcome of this scheme – strongly suggests that failure to enforce the law has rendered its deterrent function completely ineffectual. The prevention of crime and the maintenance of good order in society are thus presented as virtually equivalent to each other, making the deterrent function of the law thematically central to the play:

> Now, as fond fathers,
> Having bound up the threatening twigs of birch,
> Only to stick it in their children's sight
> For terror, not to use, in time the rod
> Becomes more mocked than feared; so our decrees,
> Dead to infliction, to themselves are dead,
> And liberty plucks justice by the nose,
> The baby beats the nurse, and quite athwart
> Goes all decorum.

(1.3.23–31)

Parental figures are often prominent in Shakespearian comedies: given their conspicuous absence from this one, it is fascinating that the failure of paternal discipline is presented as the key image of social disorder in general. The Duke, the only character addressed as 'father', here seems tacitly to acknowledge his responsibility for the state of Vienna. Presenting the family and the state as images of one another is a common trope of patriarchal social theory in the early modern period. In this light, the getting of children outside the framework of the legally sanctioned family poses an important symbolic threat to social order, and Claudio and Juliet's relationship becomes more than a matter of personal morality. It is not surprising, then, that one of

15

the first acts of the new regime is to carry out the public shaming of Claudio as he is taken off to prison. Commanded 'by special charge' from Angelo (1.2.111), this feature of his punishment clearly implies that his fate is supposed to have a deterrent effect, using the street theatre of ritual humiliation to issue a threatening lesson in public morality.

As the events of the play unfold, however, the dramatic focus shifts away from the Duke's strange scheme to reform the legal and social order in Vienna, and onto the need to deal with the extraordinary results that flow from it. Consequently, the retributive and reformative functions of the legal system come to be of central concern. The first of these is most obviously demonstrated by Angelo's wholehearted commitment to capital punishment, but is also exemplified by the punitive attitude he reveals when he says to Escalus, of Pompey and Froth, 'I'll take my leave,/And leave you to the hearing of the cause,/Hoping you'll find good cause to whip them all' (2.1.130–2). But the penal system's mission to reform, to make bad subjects into good ones, is most vividly illustrated by Pompey's transformation from bawd to hangman. The irony of this change is nicely demonstrated by Pompey's own reflections, at once comic and critical, on the collision of reform and retribution in his new occupation: 'Sir, I have been an unlawful bawd time out of mind, but yet I will be content to be a lawful hangman…I do find your hangman is a more penitent trade than your bawd; he doth oftener ask forgiveness' (4.2.14–15, 47–9). The distinction between the retributive and the reformative underlies the play's central engagement with the ethics of justice and mercy, and is played out most dramatically in the final scene, where the Duke's initial insistence that Angelo must share the same fate as Claudio is tempered by the pleas for mercy put up by Mariana and Isabella.

Measure for Measure stages a theatrical encounter with questions of law, punishment, and their relation to social order that were undergoing considerable change in Shakespeare's society. Pieter Spierenburg, a historian of prisons and punishment in early modern Europe, traces a movement away from forms of corporal punishment (such as the whippings that are repeatedly threatened but never performed in *Measure for Measure*) towards

16

bondage or incarceration, and argues that this shift was bound up with several social and cultural processes.[9] These include the increasing privatization of some aspects of daily life that had formerly been treated as relatively public; the emergence of new attitudes to the body; a growing sensitivity in relation to violence; and changes in the nature and role of the family. This last point was particularly important, as criminals were often viewed as having failed to respond to the processes of socialization and moral instruction that the family was supposed to carry out, or having in some way eluded or resisted its disciplinary bonds. We have already seen that the Duke shares this understanding of the origins of criminality. For this reason, prisoners were subjected to a quasi-patriarchal discipline modelled on that which should be found in the ideal family. Since imprisonment nearly always involved forced labour, it was thought to be well suited to the reformation of criminals, who would benefit from the therapeutic effects of regular, productive work, and would learn through labour to be responsible members of society. Incarceration designed to reform the criminal was thus directed particularly at those who, prone to idleness and immorality, were guilty of indulging in an entire lifestyle that required correction. In their different ways, Lucio and Pompey are both prime candidates: as the Duke says of the latter, 'Correction and instruction must both work/ Ere this rude beast will profit' (3.1.300–1).

Correction and instruction were also available to the equivalents of Lucio and Pompey in Shakespeare's London, at the Bridewell, within the city walls on Fleet Street, but still only a short walk away from the Liberties, the districts where theatres and brothels flourished. According to its Ordinances, the London Bridewell was established in the mid-sixteenth century 'to be a workhouse for the poor and idle persons of London, that our old sore of idleness may no longer grieve the commonwealth ... to compel the idle strumpet and vagabond to honest exercize, so the lewd and the idle should remain to labour so long as they were whole, and not be set at liberty on the highways'.[10] Setting up the Bridewell, London's city fathers declared 'the mean [sic] to reform beggary is to fall to work'; the rationale of the 1576 Act was that in houses of correction 'youth may be accustomed and brought up in labour and work, and

17

then not like to grow to be idle rogues'. Sir Edward Coke, the seventeenth-century legal theorist who played a major role in shaping what was to become the modern British legal system, thought that Bridewells were effective, remarking, 'few are committed to the House of Correction or Working-House, but they come out better'. But there was a penal element, as well as the reformative: a plan for a Westminster Bridewell in 1561 said that one aim was the 'repressing of the idle, sturdy vagabond and common strumpet', and the statutes of 1576, 1597, and 1610 all listed punishment as an aim. The fact that the usual regime combined whipping with incarceration and hard labour bears this out. In one house of correction, all prisoners were chained or manacled in some way; refusal to work was punished by further whipping, shackling, or 'thinner diet and hard labour'; conversely, extra rations were offered as an incentive to work.[11]

The early modern prison was not, therefore, merely a place where punishments were inflicted on wrongdoers, but a house of correction where, through labour and the kind of moral manipulation practised by the Duke on Claudio and the Provost on Barnardine, they were to be re-formed as productive, responsible members of society. In *Measure for Measure*, Pompey is told that his old-style corporal punishments will be mitigated if he accepts the appropriation of his labour in the service of the new penal regime. He seems to be a willing participant in this process, embarking on his new role as hangman with gusto, illustrated by the cheery mock-civility with which he addresses Barnardine on the morning appointed for the latter's execution (4.3.20–44). Lucio, though, remains resistant: in the fact of the Duke's insistence that he must marry 'any woman . . . /Whom he begot with child' (5.1.512, 514), he complains that this is an excessive punishment, as bad as combining all the resources of the old penal regime in one. The Duke is trying to use the structure of comic drama to institute his reformatory moral regime, deploying to social and moral ends the traditional happy ending in which the characters troop off stage two by two to embark on their multiple marriages. But Lucio will not submit himself to the Duke's dramatic manipulations. Indeed, his response to his sentence undermines the whole notion that in comedy marriage is a happy ending, for he views it as a distinctly unhappy outcome. In his misogynist lament that

'Marrying a punk, my lord, is pressing to death, whipping, and hanging' (5.1.520–1), he does not present marriage as a desirable alternative to death, but as essentially equivalent to death. Curiously, Lucio is often seconded in this by modern readers and audiences who, on first encounter with the play, are dismayed by the Duke's phrase 'And see our pleasure herein executed' (5.1.520), which they take to mean that Lucio will indeed be put to death. There is a darkly comic irony in this phrase, certainly, which seems all too appropriate in a play where sex and death are so closely connected, and where the deaths that conventionally conclude tragic dramas are so belatedly commuted to marriage. It also evokes Isabella's startling reaction, on first hearing the history of Angelo and Mariana's liaisons from the Duke, when she sees death rather than marriage as the ideal outcome to their situation: 'What a merit were it in death to take this poor maid from the world! What corruption in this life, that it will let this man live!' (3.1.233–5). Likewise, though stopping short of wanting to see Mariana dead, modern theatregoers are often reluctant to accept her marriage to Angelo as part of a happy ending, finding it hard to project beyond the end of the play into a happy-ever-after for this couple whose marriage begins so unpromisingly.

So far, I have focused almost entirely on the encounter of male characters with the civic and legal institutions of Vienna. But there is at least one female prisoner, who, though largely silent, plays a central role in the drama. Juliet's first appearance in Act 1 Scene 2 is oddly speechless and passive: though the audience's attention is drawn to her entrance by Pompey's 'there's Madam Juliet' (1.2.107), no lines are scripted for her, and no stage direction provides her with an exit. What, then, is her function in this scene? Certainly, to present Claudio alone at this point, introducing Juliet only for her interview with the Duke in Act 2 Scene 3, the only scene where she speaks, would be odd. Moreover, Claudio's objection to being publicly displayed rather than taken directly to prison ('Fellow, why dost thou show me thus to the world?' (1.2.108)) suggests that he and Juliet may be undergoing a punishment involving ritualized humiliation, of the kind frequently inflicted on sexual offenders in Shakespeare's time. Peter Brook's celebrated 1950 staging of *Measure*

19

for Measure with the Royal Shakespeare Company at Stratford-upon-Avon brought this out forcefully, crowding the stage with a rumbustious throng of people, the inhabitants of low-life Vienna, who bore dismayed witness to the public shaming of Claudio and Juliet. Social historians have shown how early modern cultures used public shaming punishments to regulate behaviour around gender and sexuality. Drawing on this work, Victoria Hayne argues that in *Measure for Measure* a theatrical version of such a ritual is performed: the humiliating public penance of Act 1, Scene 2, is followed, in the Duke's interviews of Claudio and Juliet in prison, by the confession and reconciliation to the law that the punishment was designed to elicit. Laura Lungers Knopper also uses historical evidence concerning women punished publicly for sexual transgressions in relation to *Measure for Measure*, although for her the shaming ritual is to be found in the final scene, where first Isabella and then Mariana are forced to confess to being, in the proverbial phrase used by the Duke and echoed by Lucio, 'neither maid, widow, nor wife' (5.1.176–9).

In modern performances, when Juliet appears in Act 1, Scene 2, the juxtaposition of her silence with her conspicuously pregnant body is eloquent and important in terms of the play's insistence on the meaningfulness and legibility of women's bodies. Sometimes she is kept on stage, under guard, a mute witness to the conflicts of morality, sexuality, and power played out before her, and a painful reminder to the audience of what is at stake. In the 1975 RSC production her hair was roughly cut short as a sign of criminalized status; twenty years later, at the same theatre, she was shackled, gagged, and closely guarded. Juliet's body is the sign of the crime: the reciprocal secret pleasures that she and Claudio enjoyed are betrayed by the indiscretion of the female body, disclosed in a key metaphor: 'The stealth of our most mutual entertainment/With character too gross is writ on Juliet' (1.2.152–3). When her return to the stage is scripted by Shakespeare, some sixty lines before the end of the play, she is equally speechless, but again her physical presence may be full of meaning. Directors often show her carrying in her arms a newly-born child: the sin she carried is here transformed into an embodied image of the fertility so lyrically celebrated by Lucio in his interview with Isabella earlier in the play:

20

Your brother and his lover have embraced.
As those that feed grow full, as blossoming time
That from the seedness the bare fallow brings
To teeming foison, even so her plenteous womb
Expresseth his full tilth and husbandry.

(1.4.39–43)

Such a stage spectacle undermines the sexual ideology of the
Duke's question, 'Repent you, fair one, of the sin you carry?'
(2.3.19), put to Juliet in an attempt to enforce a double standard
of sexual behaviour for men and women, and which even at the
time of asking is cast in doubt by her ambivalent response: 'I do
repent me as it is an evil,/And take the shame with joy' (2.3.35–
6). Though the Duke seems satisfied with this response, it can
easily be read as indicating resistance to the moral scheme he is
trying to impose. The role of Juliet, then, can be staged in a way
that helps to replace reproductive sexuality as a positive value in
a world that had constructed sexuality purely as a matter of
commodification, crime, and exchange – whether the transaction be commercial, as in the brothel, or directed to the ends that
Mariana's dark encounter with Angelo achieved. In the cases of
both Claudio–Juliet and Mariana–Angelo, it is the absence of a
dowry that prevents the completion of the marriage process,
underlining the extent to which marriage in this society is not
merely a matter of love and affection, but also a transaction
based in property, as the words of the Duke's proposal to
Isabella illustrate:

Dear Isabel,
I have a motion much imports your good,
Whereto if you'll a willing ear incline,
What's mine is yours, and what is yours is mine.

(5.1.533–6)

Like the earlier comment on women who are 'neither maid,
widow, nor wife', the Duke's phrasing here is proverbially
inspired. Proverbs often work to express or uphold traditional,
conservative ways of making sense of the world. Whatever we
think of the marriages that feature in this final scene of the play,
marriage, both as property arrangement and as affective
relation, was undoubtedly a crucial pillar of the social order of
early modern England. This centrality had important conse-

21

quences for the standards by which the sexual morality of individuals was assessed. Martha Widmayer has argued that *Measure for Measure* reflects the period's interest in regulating personal conduct as an aspect of maintaining social order.[12] This connection between the regulation of personal conduct and the maintenance of social order was partly based on the assumptions that the able-bodied poor must be poor as a result of wasting their time and money on loose living, and that poverty and the desire to continue their wicked ways would inevitably drive them to crime. Such assumptions clearly underlie the foundation at this time of a corrective penal regime centrally concerned with the therapeutic power of forced labour, dramatized in *Measure for Measure* through the roles of Pompey and Lucio. Though the notion of personal conduct was by no means exclusively sexual, one of the concerns of this movement for the reformation of manners was, Widmayer argues, with bastardy. The reformation of manners was in many respects less a moral movement than an economic and political one, concerned with adjudicating between the needs and responsibilities of the individual and the community. In cases of illegitimate birth, one of the key issues was always how the child's material needs were to be met. In *Measure for Measure*, this is illustrated by Lucio's comment on the Duke, 'Ere he would have hanged a man for the getting a hundred bastards, he would have paid for the nursing a thousand. He had some feeling of the sport; he knew the service, and that instructed him to mercy' (3.1.380–4), which in its comic overstatement conjures up a ludicrous picture of the Duke as a man who sows his wild oats on a grand scale. More seriously, it evokes the state's responsibility for the keep of illegitimate children; in this light, Mrs Overdone's care for Lucio and Kate Keepdown's bastard casts her as a socially responsible citizen to whom the Duke should be grateful, rather than punitive. Since Mrs Overdone's fate at the end of the play is left unclear, it is probably just as well that Lucio is to be forced to marry and shoulder his responsibilities, or the parish would be liable for his child at least – though his speeches repeatedly stress the procreative aspect of human sexuality, he is casual about his own procreative pleasures. Though Lucio's subversive, mobile, witty presence recommends him to modern audiences, his callous, irresponsible attitude towards Kate Keepdown and their child perhaps constitutes an argument for resisting his seductive charms. In a play where characters are repeatedly required to pass judgment on others in the light of their own behaviour, he is in no position, in the biblical phrase, to cast the first stone at the Duke.

2

The Scene Vienna

Some of Shakespeare's plays advertise their location in their title: *The Merchant of Venice*, *The Merry Wives of Windsor*, *The Tragedy of Hamlet, Prince of Denmark*. *Measure for Measure* bears a label that identifies its location explicitly in a different way. In the First Folio of Shakespeare's plays, the closing lines of the play are, unusually, followed by a terse designation of its setting: 'The Scene Vienna'. There is only one other reference to Vienna in all of Shakespeare's works – perhaps ominously, *Hamlet*'s play within a play, 'The Murder of Gonzago', is set there. *Measure for Measure* is one of just two plays in the Folio whose location is pinned down by such a label (the other is *The Tempest*, located on 'an uninhabited island'), and scholars have suggested that these uncharacteristically precise locations were contributed not by Shakespeare but by Ralph Crane, the man who prepared transcripts of these plays for publication. But this need not imply that the Folio's insistence on the Viennese setting of the play is irrelevant or insignificant. There is much within the play-text that reminds us that the location is Vienna: characters mention the name of the city repeatedly, especially in the first few scenes, and references to Hungary, Poland, Bohemia, and Russia would also have encouraged Shakespeare's London audience to feel that the action of this play occurs at the farther edge of Europe, in a country both like and unlike their own.

Shakespeare's stage did not represent particular places or evoke their atmosphere through the use of scenery; but this does not mean that a sense of place was unimportant. Instead of the visual clues provided by scenery and costume, it is through language that the audience is given information about where the play is set, and what meanings this choice of location brings

Fig. 3. Measure for Measure was a popular subject for illustration by
Pre-Raphaelite artists: E. A. Abbey depicts a melancholic
Mariana listening to a boy singer who is blind as Cupid.

Ivan Kyncl

Fig. 4. Mariana (Tanya Moodie) reveals herself to Vienna's patriarchs in the 1994 RSC production directed by Steven Pimlott.

with it: most obviously the title, but also the dialogue (Viola's haunting query, 'What country, friends, is this?', drawing the response 'This is Illyria, lady' (*Twelfth Night*, 1.2.1–2)), and the implied stage directions embedded within it (Ulysses' remark that 'Achilles stands i'th' entrance of his tent', (*Troilus and Cressida*, 3.3.38)). The famous lines of the Chorus that open *Henry V* emphasize the importance of a sense of theatrical place, even where location cannot be demonstrated on stage, and demand the audience's complicity in conjuring up an imaginary vision of the places of that play:

> Can this cock-pit hold
> The vasty fields of France? Or may we cram
> Within this wooden O the very casques
> That did affright the air at Agincourt?
> O pardon: since a crooked figure may
> Attest in little place a million,
> And let us, ciphers to this great account,
> On your imaginary forces work.

(Henry V, Prologue, 11–18)

How, then, does *Measure for Measure*'s setting in Vienna work on the 'imaginary forces' of the theatregoer or reader?

In opting for Vienna as a location, Shakespeare seems to have been influenced by his two main sources, a 1565 tale by the Italian writer Giraldi Cinthio set in Innsbruck (now in Austria, but at that time, like Vienna, part of the Holy Roman Empire), and George Whetstone's play *The Historie of Promos and Cassandra* (1578), which occurs in a fictional middle-European city under the control of the King of Hungary and Bohemia. Shakespeare only rarely uses locations in central or Eastern Europe for his plays, and when he does they tend to have an unreal, somewhat fairy-tale quality. Like Illyria in *Twelfth Night* or the coast of Bohemia in *The Winter's Tale*, the main point about such settings is that they are distant, elsewhere. On the other hand, in the case of *Measure for Measure* numerous critics have argued that, by setting his play in a city that is ostensibly not-here, Shakespeare actually freed himself to represent the here and now of his London in disguised form, opening up the possibility of commenting on the political, moral, and social life of the city without fear of direct challenge or censorship. But even if the life that boils and bubbles in Vienna's prisons, convents, and public spaces does seem to bear an uncanny similarity in some respects to life in Jacobean London, there are important historical factors that would have influenced a seventeenth-century audience's understanding that this fictional Vienna both was and was not their city.

If visitors from Vienna had strayed into a performance of *Measure for Measure* in Jacobean London, they would have recognized few details of the setting as characteristic of their home. But for English members of the audience, the mere act of naming the city would evoke a range of cultural associations. In her detailed study of the topical meanings of *Measure for Measure*, Leah Marcus notes that Vienna, as one of the capitals of the Holy Roman Empire and the seat of the immensely powerful Habsburg dynasty, was 'the administrative hub of a vast and shifting Catholic alliance with which the English had been on hostile terms for decades'.[1] The Habsburg Empire and its alliances extended through much of central Europe, down into Spain as well as northward to the Netherlands. Marcus claims that most of the playgoers of Protestant London in 1604 would have perceived Vienna in the context of anxieties about the Holy Roman Empire's expansionary tendencies. Mentioning this distant city would evoke fears of a further extension of Habsburg domination, bringing in its wake imperial repression and the inquisitorial, perhaps bloody, reimposition of Catholicism. Thus the discussion of peace negotiations involving the Duke of Vienna, 'the other Dukes', and the King of Hungary in Act 1, Scene 2, may play on anxieties about the likely fate of Protestants in Hungary, whose perilous situation in 1604 was being carefully observed by English sympathizers. Rumours in the closing years of Elizabeth I's reign that the Archduke Albert and his wife Isabella would seek to claim the English throne, and to this end were sending to England secret agents, often in the guise of priests and friars, can have done nothing to allay such anxieties.

Let me take one specific example of how the details of the play can be interpreted in this historical context. Anxieties about the possible encroachment of the Holy Roman Empire, accompanied by paranoid fears about the presence of Catholic secret agents in England, can help to explain the moment at 5.1.308 when the threat of judicial violence suddenly and shockingly erupts. It is all the more startling because it is the previously moderate,

26

sympathetic Escalus who demands that Friar Lodowick be taken to prison and tortured on the rack, warning him, 'We'll touse you/Joint by joint.' Though corporal punishment (the whippings offered to Pompey and Lucio) and psychological manipulation (the Provost's repeated pretences that the hour for Barnardine's execution has come) are referred to elsewhere in the play, this is the only mention of torture as such. It seems not to be part of the general penal regime, but rather a special measure called for by the sense that this 'unreverent and unhallowed friar' (5.1.302) is an outsider, come to Vienna with a sinister 'purpose' (5.1.309) that prompts him to suborn its inhabitants to join him in committing 'slander to the state' (5.1.320) and 'treasonable abuses' (5.1.340). It is implied, then, that the Friar's mission to Vienna is politically motivated, involving espionage and sedition. Thus he is not a common criminal but a special case, meriting especially brutal treatment. In Chapter 1, I discussed the links between political power and the law. In this brief glimpse of the severity meted out to those presumed guilty of attempting to subvert the state, the potential of the penal system to be used in the service of the political aims of the state, as well as its importance as a means of maintaining social order in all its forms, are underlined.

Fears of a Catholic resurgence linked to a Habsburg attempt to claim the throne were effectively allayed by James VI of Scotland's accession, under the title of James I, to the unified throne of England, Wales, and Scotland on Elizabeth's death in 1603. But the need to come to better terms with the Habsburg Empire remained a political reality. To this end the Treaty of London, signalling the reconciliation of James's realm with the Habsburgs, was signed in the summer of 1604. *Measure for Measure* had its first performance at court a few months later, and Leah Marcus suggests that this fact permits an interpretation of the play as propaganda for the Treaty of London's attempt to shift the basis of British relations with the most powerful forces of Catholic Europe. Interpreting the play in this way requires audiences to see the Duke as 'wise and compassionate – a model of virtuous government according to the principles of James I himself.'[2] In fact, the desire to perceive the Duke not just as a ruler who governs on Jamesian principles, but as an idealized version of James himself, has recurred in

27

interpretations of the play, as I indicated in the previous chapter. However, not everyone has been prepared to see the Duke in such a favourable light. And there are more general problems – as Marcus acknowledges – with this kind of meticulously topical approach, which runs the risk of implying that a unique key to the true meaning of the play can be found in the decoding of concealed or indirect references to contemporary events. It is important to recall that, over the past four centuries, *Measure for Measure*, like most of Shakespeare's plays, has generated a wide range of divergent critical responses. Some of these differences result from the changing cultural and historical contexts in which the play has been interpreted; but it seems reasonable to assume that the 1604 audience may also have held diverse views about the play's meanings. Nor should we give undue emphasis to the fact that the first recorded performance of *Measure for Measure* took place at court, allowing ourselves to be swayed by this into seeing the play exclusively through the eyes of royal strategists. International diplomacy was not of interest to all, and popular response to the Treaty of London appears to have been lukewarm.

Moreover, though no record exists of *Measure for Measure* being performed in the London public theatre during Shakespeare's lifetime, this does not mean that no such performance took place, as the records are not wholly complete and reliable. In fact, the ordinary practice of his company, the King's Men, was to perform their plays both at court and in the commercial theatre. This certainly suggests that the aristocracy and the theatregoing public might share some common tastes, but it does not exclude the possibility of differences between and among these audiences, as Louis Montrose usefully reminds us: 'Shakespeare's plays played to both courtly and popular audiences, and these audiences constituted frequently overlapping but nevertheless distinct and potentially contradictory sources of socioeconomic support and constraint.'[3] Members of a courtly audience, diplomats and soldiers whose lives were entangled with the shifting alliances of the great powers in Europe, might well have found the search for topical resonance an absorbing and important way of understanding the play. But other spectators, more preoccupied with religion, sex, or money, would have viewed the play differently – and the same can, of course, be said for all of *Measure for Measure*'s subsequent audiences.

The question of religion is particularly intriguing. In the Introduction, I touched on the difficulties associated with analysing such a thoroughly Christian play in an age like ours, where the status of religious belief and practice is in flux. But I should perhaps have emphasized more strongly to what extent this was also true in Shakespeare's time. In outlining Leah Marcus's topical interpretation of *Measure for Measure*, I have proceeded as if all members of an English audience would have been Protestants, unproblematically united in their fear and loathing of Catholic realms such as the Holy Roman Empire. But it is, of course, far too simplistic to assume that all Protestants would have shared the same views. Moreover, despite the persecutions that had intermittently followed the Reformation that led to the establishment of Protestantism as the state-sanctioned religion in England, there was still a substantial, though cautious and secretive, Catholic minority there. Indeed, a number of scholars have recently made a persuasive case for believing that Shakespeare himself may have been a Catholic.[4]

Whatever Shakespeare's personal beliefs may have been, it is clear that *Measure for Measure* does not allow its audience to hold rigidly hostile attitudes towards Catholics. Nor are the references to Catholic institutions merely part of the paraphernalia of distance and exoticism in the play. The Viennese setting allows Shakespeare to draw on certain aspects of the Catholic religion for dramatic effect: the Duke's disguise as a Friar permits him a good deal of social and spatial mobility, helps to make the fact that no one in Vienna recognizes their disguised ruler credible, and provides him with the opportunity both to elicit confessions from and offer authoritative advice to people whom he needs to manipulate. Similarly, Isabella's status as a young woman who has chosen to embrace the poverty, chastity, and obedience that are fundamental to life in a convent serves to sharpen the pain and terror of the situation in which Angelo places her. The play simply will not work unless an audience is prepared to take features like these seriously: a monolithically Protestant audience united in hatred and scorn for all things Catholic could make very little sense, and gain scarcely any pleasure, from this play. Thus, although the audience will no doubt bring with them into the theatre all sorts of baggage concerning themselves and their world, and will make sense of the play in the light of those concerns, Shakespearian drama requires that they also enter willingly into the fictional world of the play, temporarily suspending their usual priorities and preoccupations. This is what allows the play to remain dynamic and theatrically alive, enabling audiences in different places at different times to find something of themselves in it, but also to experience the pleasure and terror of being taken out of themselves, out of the world they inhabit.

More recently, Vienna has taken on a set of associations that have a distinctive significance for *Measure for Measure*. As the city where, in the closing years of the nineteenth century and the opening decades of the twentieth, Sigmund Freud saw his patients, collaborated with other doctors, and wrote some of the most influential books of modern times, Vienna has become identified as the birthplace of psychoanalysis. Though it has been challenged and contested from many points of view, psychoanalysis has undoubtedly provided the modern world with a set of terms and concepts – repression, the unconscious, the Oedipus complex, for example – that have passed into everyday use, and with a way of interpreting human behaviour that has been extraordinarily influential. Shakespeare's Vienna, like Freud's – and perhaps also like Shakespeare's London – is a turn-of-the-century city where moral values and social practices are subject to change. In psychoanalytic thought and in the world of Shakespeare's play, sexual desire is perceived to be a crucial motivating force in human behaviour, and one that needs to be managed carefully in relation to the needs of society. Neither free expression of sexual desire, nor its total repression, seem to be effective: what *Measure for Measure* requires, and psychoanalysis describes, is a society based on the sublimation of desire – that is, the channeling of erotic energies in socially acceptable ways.

Theatre directors have sometimes chosen to set *Measure for Measure* in a Vienna which seems to be more Freud's city than Shakespeare's: in Canada in 1975, for example, the director Robin Philips located the play in Vienna in 1912, and gave it an explicitly Freudian emphasis. Justifying this decision, he remarked 'I would not be surprised to find that Freud or Ibsen were devoted to *Measure for Measure'*. Unfortunately, there is no evidence to suggest that this was the case, although generally Freud was devoted to Shakespeare. He recommended that aspiring psychoanalysts should study literature as part of their training, and more than once claimed that 'The poets and philosophers discovered the unconscious before I did'.[5] In several instances his meditations on Shakespeare's plays had a formative role in the development of key psychoanalytic ideas – in his early thinking about what came to be known as the Oedipus complex, for example, it was to *Hamlet* and not to the plays of Sophocles that he turned. Since Freud's time, psycho-analysis has proved enormously fruitful for both academic and theatrical interpretations of Shakespeare. But it has not gone unchallenged. In her book on *Measure for Measure* Harriett Hawkins dismisses the relevance of psychoanalysis to the play, arguing that the 'sexual, social and emotional problems posed in *Measure for Measure* are [not] amenable to solution-by-diagnosis in Freudian terms'.[6] Her reservations are understandable, for it has to be acknowledged that *Measure for Measure* has sometimes been the subject of psychoanalytic readings that have inter-preted it in rather reductive ways. Some psychoanalytically influenced critics tend to speak of the characters as if they are real people, complete with emotional prehistories that Shake-speare may have imagined but for which the scripts provide us with no evidence. This approach can produce interpretations that appear unintentionally comic or lurid in their depiction of troubled psyches and thwarted desires.

Carolyn E. Brown's interesting attempt to combine a twentieth-century psychoanalytic understanding of human personality with an understanding of the historical importance of religious beliefs and practices in Shakespeare's time ambitiously tackles issues that are central to the play. But it becomes somewhat overheated when she addresses the topic of sexual repression: 'Though the protagonists [Angelo, the Duke, Isabella] try to convince themselves that they have killed their libidos, they store within themselves a time bomb of danger-ously active and unacknowledged libidos, diseased and intensified by too severe constraints, which surreptitiously strive for gratification.'[7] Rather than being perceived as participants in a drama whose dénouement will be shaped by a whole range of political, spiritual, generic, and theatrical considerations, Shakespeare's characters are here presented as sad, sick individuals, whose problems can best be resolved not by the happy ending of comic theatre, but by therapy. This kind of approach risks removing the play from the possibility of being understood in social or political terms. In Brown's essay perverse sexual desire is all-encompassing, so that *Measure for Measure*'s political focus on the institutions that deal with crime and punishment, its examination of the prison, the court, and so on, are reduced to being described as 'the morbid ambience of bondage in Vienna'.[8]

Brown concludes her essay with a detailed discussion of a notorious speech of Isabella's, which many critics have found both fascinating and problematic, where she declares:

> were I under the terms of death,
> The impression of keen whips I'd wear as rubies,
> And strip myself to death as to a bed
> That longing have been sick for, ere I'd yield
> My body up to shame.

(2.4.100–4)

In a play where the imposition of the death sentence for the crime of illicit sexuality makes terrifyingly literal the popular early modern pun that encodes orgasm as a kind of momentary death, in a fictional world where almost everyone seems acutely conscious of the close proximity of sex and death, Isabella's words are arguably unremarkable. But Brown chooses to interpret them as a sign of her personal pathology, and reads the speech by endowing Isabella with an elaborate psychological prehistory, for which the text of Shakespeare's play seems to offer sparse evidence:

Having subjected herself to severe self-denial to quell her passion, she perversely equates beating with physical desires, pain being sexually charged for her. She seems to have envisioned death so often in her bouts with passion that the two – death and lust – have become meshed, as they had for some historical flagellants, and death becomes personified as an erotic, desirable beater. Like the Duke, Isabella perversely views death in sensuous terms. She delineates the beating scene in sensuous detail, as if she has been there many times in her mind . . . she envisions on the skin the bloody stripes glowing like precious rubies.[9]

32

Brown places herself in the role of psychoanalyst, assuming that Isabella's words in the text provide a means of access to the character's imagined unconscious, and thereby a way of decoding her behaviour. To do so is to construct a secondary fiction that is then used to secure an interpretation of the fiction dramatized by Shakespeare. This kind of psychoanalytic reading closes the circuit of interpretation in a way that can furnish a very powerful and convincing account of dramatic character. However, it is important to be clear that the tendency to treat dramatic characters as if they are real people is neither exclusive to nor defining of psychoanalytic literary criticism. It is, for example, a technique that is often used very effectively by performers. Juliet Stevenson, acclaimed when she played the role of Isabella for the Royal Shakespeare Company in 1983, speaks of Isabella as if she were a real person, a friend even: someone 'whose sense of self-image is quite strong', who is 'living in her head', yet at the same time 'clued in to her sexuality'.[10] But she also describes in detail the way that the language and the silences of Shakespeare's text construct the theatrical opportunities open to the actress playing Isabella: 'there is a pulse in the verse that will tell you as much about the character as anything she says ... the language tells you who the character is moment by moment, word by word'.[11] Juliet Stevenson is an exceptionally perceptive and eloquent analyst of the relation between language and characterization in Shakespeare's plays, and her fellow-actress Paola Dionisotti expressed her admiration for Stevenson's performance as Isabella in an intriguingly sexualized metaphor, describing her as 'married to the text'.[12] So if the psychological approach to character has been criticized and challenged in recent years by scholars who find it naïve, or worry that it leaves out of account other important dimensions of the theatrical text, it still represents an honourable and influential critical tradition, which many readers, actors, and theatregoers find helpful in making sense of their responses to the human dramas Shakespeare stages.

Julia Lupton's fascinating discussion of *Measure for Measure* opens up a different way of making sense of the important and difficult moment in the play that is represented by Isabella's speech, quoted above. Lupton shares Carolyn Brown's attention to the religious dimension of the role, while reinflecting the psychoanalytic mode of interpretation of Isabella to offer an original and convincing account that places her in the context of the literary genre of hagiography, or saints' lives. Lupton argues that Isabella's journey through the play echoes the trajectory of female martyrdom, as described in the biographies of female saints that enjoyed great popularity in the late antique and medieval periods. This trajectory moves from the heroine's renunciation of the world and embrace of chastity, through confrontation with a seductive tyrant to which the female saint mounts an eloquent self-defence, to the moment of torture and execution that is metaphorically represented in Isabella's desire to wear the 'impression of keen whips' as a badge of her virtue, and to embrace death willingly rather than submit to dishonour. Placing Shakespeare's play in dialogue with a complementary literary and historical discourse, Lupton treats Isabella's speech as a point of access not to the character's unconscious, but to what we might call the textual unconscious – the complex, uneven weave of cultural fantasies that makes this moment seem so highly charged. She approaches both *Measure for Measure* and the saints' lives she compares it with by means of the psychoanalytic method, derived from Freud's own work, of symptomatic reading – the 'symptom', here, referring to moments such as this one, that seem to point beyond themselves to something that the text is repressing, something that it cannot quite say explicitly. Lupton combines this reading strategy with an attention to context and genre in order to argue that the narrative movement of hagiography, which finds its 'happy ending' in the death of the martyr, is entirely at odds with that of secular comedy, where the heroine's end is marriage. In this light, Isabella's remarkable speech can be seen as a condensed, elliptical version of the central problem of the play itself.

Janet Adelman's influential book *Suffocating Mothers* is in many ways characteristic of a strand of psychoanalytic literary criticism that offers still further possibilities for the reading of Shakespeare. Adelman's book never considers the plays as scripts for performance, and, although it does not treat dramatic characters as patients on the couch, it does tend to endow them with autonomous psychological lives. However, she does not confine herself to a character-centred approach, but, like Julia Lupton, proceeds as if the play itself has a structure similar to that of the human psyche, with a 'textual unconscious' traversed by desires and anxieties, shaped by repression and what cannot be said as much as by what is explicitly stated or performed. This enables her to use psychoanalytic concepts to explore the dramatic construction of the play – for instance, in a demonstration of its splitting of the feminine into the two roles of Isabella and Juliet. This is dramatically illustrated by the moment in Act 2, Scene 2, where a conversation between Angelo and the Provost about how best to deal with 'the fornicatress' (2.2.23), the 'groaning Juliet' (2.2.15) who is about to go into labour, is juxtaposed with the announced arrival of the 'very virtuous maid' (2.2.20) Isabella, whose chastity is underlined by the remark that she is 'to be shortly of a sisterhood' (2.2.21). Just in case the audience has missed the point, this transition from one incarnation of femininity to another is almost immediately recapitulated in the pairing of Juliet's conversation with the Duke in Act 2, Scene 3, and Isabella's with Angelo in Act 2, scene 4. Janet Adelman eloquently analyses the wider implications of this splitting for the play's handling of female sexuality:

> Both [women's roles] derive from the same anxiety about sexuality and female generativity: the body of one – her presence mediated by Mistress Overdone, the bawd who first introduces her into the play – is the repository for the sense of sexual generation as illicit and dangerous; the body of the other – an unpolluted sanctuary about to be immured within another sanctuary – carries the promise of escape from sexuality.... But the split that initially promises to heal the sexual fault in fact reinforces it; the embodiment of sanctuary in the person of Isabella awakens the desire it would suppress.[13]

Though I am focusing in this section on the representation of female sexuality, and the use of psychoanalytic approaches to interpret women's roles, especially Isabella, psychoanalysis is of course equally relevant to the consideration of masculinity and male sexuality. Janet Adelman, for instance, counterbalances her comparison of Isabella and Juliet by similarly seeing the Duke and Angelo as a kind of Janus-faced pairing, uneasily embodying different forms of masculinity, and both representing a certain unease with women, sexuality, and the institution of marriage. One of the key insights of Cheek by Jowl's outstanding production was the sense, demonstrated in the performances of Stephen Boxer as the Duke and Adam Kotz as Angelo, that the substitution of Angelo for the Duke as the city's ruler is rooted in the fact that they are 'two sides of the same puritan coin',[14] twinned in their desire for control and in their desire for Isabella.

One of the most distinctive, and historically most controversial, aspects of psychoanalytic theory is its understanding of human sexuality as essentially blind, amoral, and self-serving – an understanding that is shared by Shakespearian comedies. Katherine Eisaman Maus comments on the 'primary irony of sexual desire: that the lover's vivid conviction – or illusion – of the beloved's uniqueness conflicts with a kind of *eros* perhaps best described as depersonalized genital attraction'.[15] The farcical interchangeability of objects of desire in *A Midsummer Night's Dream* is an obvious illustration of this phenomenon, but it also seems to underlie the use of the theatrical device known as the 'bed-trick' in both *Measure for Measure* and *All's Well That Ends Well*, two plays that date from the same phase of Shakespeare's career. This undiscriminating quality to (particularly male) sexuality was designated in Shakespeare's time by the proverbial statement that 'Joan is as good as my lady in the dark'. Since Joan was a name associated in popular culture with women of the servant class, difference of rank is inscribed in this phrase, as it frequently is in theatrical uses of the bed-trick. This is the case in *All's Well That Ends Well*, though not *Measure for Measure*, where Mariana is not obviously of different social rank from the other characters. She is, though, left socially vulnerable by the death of her brother and Angelo's desertion, and her awkwardly liminal social status is dramatically figured by her isolation at the moated grange. Perhaps it is this vulnerable liminality – shared by Isabella, although it takes different forms for her – that generates the unease many people feel at the moral implications of the bed-trick in *Measure for Measure*. Certainly, the Duke's plan to entrap Angelo using Mariana and Isabella as his pawns produces a very different impression from the bed-trick in *All's Well That Ends Well*, which is planned and executed by the women it most nearly concerns, representatives of what Angela Carter called the resourceful girls of folklore, who deploy riddles and disguise to achieve the goal of marriage.[16] With this theatrical device, *Measure for Measure* marks the limits of the usefulness of psychologistic criticism, as the play shifts momentarily out of the Vienna that bears certain affinities with both Freud's city and Shakespeare's London, and briefly occupies the timeless, placeless realm of folklore.

Such contrasting interpretations of Isabella's role show that Harriett Hawkins's claim that producing a Freudian reading of a Shakespeare play is equivalent to attaching diagnostic labels to the characters' personal problems is too simple. In critical practice, psychoanalytic approaches to Shakespeare's plays have been very diverse, and have served to open up a range of ways to enhance our understanding of this play that is so obviously saturated in the central concerns of psychoanalysis: desire, death, and anxiety. Jacqueline Rose argues for the usefulness of psychoanalysis to the interpretation of literature, particularly with respect to texts where representations of gender and sexuality are important, on the grounds that psychoanalysis and literature share 'a terrain of language, fantasy, and sexuality – a terrain in which the woman occupies a crucial, but difficult, place'.[17] She traces the critical history of *Measure for Measure* in the twentieth century in order to argue that, for many critics whose attitudes to female sexuality are shaped by patriarchal preconceptions, the character of Isabella comes to be located as a site within the play of something that is disturbing in both sexual and aesthetic terms: 'In the critical debates about Isabella, it is as if we can see anxiety about aesthetic or representational cohesion turning into a sexual approach.'[18] And, of course, the converse is also true: conflicted views about Isabella's sexuality – or perhaps it is better to say, her chastity – provoke critics to hold it responsible for the play's artistic and structural defects.

A key question that is often posed by critics interpreting the speech where Isabella expresses her willingness to submit her body to 'th'impression of keen whips' (2.4.101) is whether or not she registers the sexual implications of her words. Within the context of an approach that attributes psychological interiority to dramatic characters, whether we choose to assume that she is in control of her rhetoric or betraying her unconscious desires and anxieties will make a considerable difference to our sense of her character in general. Here, the critic has to consider whether she or he wants to be complicit with the sense shared by Angelo, Claudio, and Lucio that Isabella's body speaks more eloquently than her words can. In imaging her moral existence in such fleshly, erotic terms, is she deliberately deploying a rhetoric equivalent to theirs, or being betrayed by it? Claudio's description of Isabella's 'prone and speechless dialect/Such as may move men' (1.2.171–2) when he asks Lucio to take a message to her is the first attempt to represent Isabella as someone whose body may be eloquent and seductive in ways that exceed what she knows or desires. Lucio's understanding of the power of this body language is demonstrated when he urges her to intensify her onslaught on Angelo: 'to him again, entreat him,/Kneel down before him, hang upon his gown' (2.2.43–4). That this strategy is all too effective is revealed in Angelo's soliloquizing after Isabella's departure (2.2.168–92). When Isabella returns to Angelo to find out his decision in Act 2, Scene 4, her opening words constitute what he recognizes as an inadvertent pun, perhaps indicating that 'this virtuous maid' (2.2.190) has to some extent internalized the men's perception of her:

ISABELLA I am come to know your pleasure.
ANGELO That you might know it would much better please me
Than to demand what 'tis.

(2.4.31–3)

For the audience, the intervening scene's staging of Juliet's pregnant body, the visible sign of her sexual crime, has underlined the eroticization of female embodiment in which Claudio, Lucio, and Angelo are all complicit. But Isabella seeks to resist this, placing her body in opposition to her soul in order to refuse these attempts to make her into a second Juliet:

ANGELO Which had you rather: that the most just law
Now took your brother's life, or, to redeem him,
Give up your body to such sweet uncleanness
As she that he hath stained?
ISABELLA   Sir, believe this.
I had rather give my body than my soul.

(2.4.52–6)

38

The collapse of Isabella's attempt to defend her spiritual and physical integrity in the face of Angelo's insistence that only by yielding up her body to his will can she save her brother leads her to the point of desperation articulated in the shattering couplet that is uttered at the very centre of the play, 'Then Isabel live chaste, and brother die/More than our brother is our chastity' (2.4.184–5). With this statement, Isabella unknowingly places herself in stark opposition to Claudio's willingness to exploit the eloquence of her embodied femininity. Isabella's insistence on the overriding value of her chastity is the pivot on which the plot turns, but many readers have found its moral and emotional implications as hard to accept as Claudio does. Isabella's only soliloquy ends with this declaration and her consequent determination to go to Claudio and tell him to 'fit his mind to death' (2.4.187). As a result, she is nowhere given the opportunity to explain or justify her position. The paucity of soliloquies does not diminish the theatrical power of the role of Isabella: indeed, the obligation placed on the actress to convey a range of complex ideas and intense emotions with only the briefest of opportunities to address herself directly to the audience is a key part of the role's challenge and excitement. But, as I have argued, in interpreting Isabella theatrical matters easily become overlaid with moral concerns, and simplistic moralizing has often rushed in to fill the silence created by the marked decrease in the number of lines Isabella is given in the second half of the play. The Christian critic G. Wilson Knight, for example, adopted an unpleasantly leering tone to suggest that Isabella's apparent commitment to chastity was actually rooted in a disturbed, pathological sexuality: 'Her sex inhibitions have been horribly shown her as they are, naked. She has been stung – lanced on a sore spot of her soul.'[19]

In almost all the source stories, the Isabella character does have sex with the corrupt deputy, and eventually marries him, thereby wiping clean the sexual stain on her social identity. The difference in Shakespeare's version is that Isabella is not a private individual but a woman who has chosen to embrace chastity as a vocation, as a way of life that marks her off as separated from the world in which Claudio, Lucio, and Angelo all live. Her refusal to save Claudio's life by submitting to

Angelo's 'concupiscible intemperate lust' (5.1.98) thus needs to be understood in terms not so much of her sexuality, as of her status as probationer to the sisterhood of St Clare. As member of a religious community and as Claudio's sibling, Isabella is a sister in two senses, and these two senses are at war with each other. In a fictional world where sexuality is either equated with death, to the extent that Claudio himself views his impending death as an erotic encounter – 'If I must die,/I will encounter darkness as a bride,/And hug it in mine arms' (3.1.81–3) – or perceived solely in terms of the life-giving pregnancies that result from it, Isabella's indifference to the life-and-death stakes placed on her chastity represents an entirely different set of values. From the earliest days of the Church, one strand of Christianity has sought to separate itself from the world and the cycles of sex, birth, and death that sustain human society, seeking through chastity and self-mortification to subdue the body and silence desire. This ascetic renunciation of the world and the flesh informs the arguments used by both Isabella and the Duke to encourage Claudio to embrace his death in Act 3, Scene 1. Though Claudio is at first compliant, he later repudiates their arguments by reasserting the centrality of the flesh to human experience, counterposing a terrifying vision of the embodied self's suffering after death:

> Ay, but to die, and go we know not where;
> To lie in cold obstruction, and to rot;
> This sensible warm motion to become
> A kneaded clod, and the dilated spirit
> To bathe in fiery floods, or to reside
> In thrilling region of thick-ribbèd ice;
> To be imprisoned in the viewless winds,
> And blown with restless violence round about
> The pendent world; or to be worse than worst
> Of those that lawless and incertain thought
> Imagine howling – 'tis too horrible!

>   (3.1.118–28)

At the beginning of the play, Isabella stands on the threshold of the convent, about to renounce the messy complications of life in the world, a renunciation that is symbolized by the chastity demanded of nuns: but the events that flow from Claudio's arrest, and his understandable reluctance to undertake a more drastic renunciation of life in the world than the one that she intends, drag her back into it. Whether she ultimately embraces the world or turns her back on it is a question to which the answer lies in the significant silences of the final scene.

This is a way of making sense of Isabella's insistence that 'More than our brother is our chastity'; but to make it intellectually comprehensible is not the same as making it emotionally and theatrically acceptable. The staging of Claudio's return from the temporary death of prison in the final scene often makes this difficulty visible. The ending of *Measure for Measure* has none of the lovely plangency of that other Shakespearian reunion of a sister with a brother apparently brought back from death, the meeting of Viola and Sebastian at the end of *Twelfth Night*. No words or gestures are scripted for Isabella's reunion with Claudio, and, though they sometimes embrace in fervent silence, it is now more common for productions to register the agonizing gulf across which their gazes meet, and to suggest that perhaps what has passed between them is beyond reconciliation. In a recent production by the French director Stéphane Braunschweig, Claudio was suddenly revealed, balanced on a ledge high above the Viennese citizens clustered on stage, naked as a newly born baby or a freshly laid-out corpse. Standing silent and immobile, on the border between death and life, he seemed, like the production's Isabella, who angrily refused the Duke's offer of marriage, to be forever set apart from society.

41

3

Houses in the Suburbs

Brothels, theatres, monasteries; hospitals, prisons, bathhouses, inns. In Chapter 1 I showed that in the early modern city single buildings could change their function over time, passing diachronically through several of the institutional uses synchronically displayed in *Measure for Measure*, with religious houses becoming theatres, and palaces being transformed into prisons. A further link between this motley set of places is that, in Shakespeare's London, they all shared a symbolically and geographically significant location at the edges of the city, in an area known as the Liberties. With the notable exception of the theatre, conspicuously absent from Shakespeare's Vienna, this list of urban sites has a good deal in common with the locations of *Measure for Measure*, which takes us to a prison and a courtroom, a convent, a moated grange, a place at the threshold of the city gates, and alludes to a holy well just outside the city, a brothel, and a walled garden. Of these places, almost none is strictly private: *Measure for Measure* is a play that essentially takes place in the public urban realm.

In an influential account, Steven Mullaney has investigated the location of theatres within the cultural geography of early modern London. He describes the Liberties as 'a geopolitical domain that was crucial to the symbolic and material economy of the city and that had traditionally been reserved for cultural phenomena that could not be contained within the strict or proper bounds of the community'.[1] For Mullaney, the significance of the location of the public theatre in the Liberties of Shakespeare's London is that for a brief time popular drama was able to appropriate the traditions of moral and cultural licence that had for centuries been maintained in the Liberties in order to achieve an ideological liberty of its own. Situated at the edges

Fig. 5. An early depiction of Mrs Overdone as a female grotesque in an 1822 illustrated edition of *Measure for Measure*.

Fig. 6. Mrs Overdone (Caroline Blakiston) and prostitutes in the 1994 RSC production.

of London, where the city butted up against the countryside, subject to the titular authority of the City of London but effectively beyond its control, the Liberties were neither quite in London nor wholly distinct from it. Excluded from the city but maintained within sight, they were a frequent destination for its inhabitants when they were in search of pleasure or destined for punishment and suffering. A marginal place that nevertheless served many vital social purposes, the Liberties marked the troublesome limits of the urban community.

Many Shakespearean dramas are structured through the juxtaposition of two worlds that represent alternative values and sets of possibilities: the place that embodies familiar, established normality, more often than not a court; and a place of licence, change, and transformation, where normal rules are suspended or called into question. This may either be a fertile site of possibility (the Forest of Arden in *As You Like It*), or a terrifying wilderness (the heath in *King Lear*). Yet the pleasurable, liberatory 'green world' is not without dangers (snakes, lions, and poverty are all to be found in the Forest of Arden), while the wilderness often proves to hold the seeds of regeneration and new hope (it is there that Lear comes to a recognition of social injustice and common human need). It has often been said that *Measure for Measure* lacks such a 'green world', remaining enclosed within the city and thereby deprived of the dangerous but fertile possibilities of the space beyond. In *Measure for Measure* there are indeed places that are not the court, that stand for other possibilities, and alternative values, but they differ from the green worlds of other comedies in being many rather than one, urban rather than rural. In other words, the places I listed at the start of this chapter, whose London equivalents would be located in the Liberties, function as Vienna's 'green world'. Indeed, the very term 'Liberties' points to the paradox of these dramatically significant locations. For the Liberties, far from being places of complete freedom, actually represent only a controlled, licensed liberation: placed at the boundaries of the normal, they serve to shore up those frontiers.

In this chapter, I want to explore these significant locations, and in particular to focus on certain kinds of place that, sharing this marginal situation, were particularly associated with women. This may help us to understand the curious place of women in

43

the world of Shakespeare's plays, insiders and outsiders, central in many ways yet often silenced and disregarded. Women's status and experience in early modern England have been the subject of a great deal of scholarly work, and in touching on the topic here I run the risk of greatly over-simplifying it.[2] What I want briefly to emphasize is the contradictory nature of women's cultural position: though they undoubtedly lived in a male-dominated society and were subjected to all sorts of prescriptions concerning their behaviour, nevertheless they were not entirely deprived of social agency. In Shakespeare's time, England was proverbially supposed to be 'the paradise of women', and, however limited or relative the truth of this may be, it has been argued that London was a place where at least some women enjoyed unusual liberty. This included the freedom to go to the public theatre, where they might often see plays like *Measure for Measure* that, by focusing their plots on matters such as love, sexuality, and marriage, reflected both women's relative freedom and the cultural anxieties it provoked.[3]

Traditionally, religious houses, like the London theatres, had tended to occupy these marginal locations. This may have been particularly true for women's religious communities. Roberta Gilchrist's important study of medieval nunneries demonstrates that convents were marginal in multiple ways: geographical, ecclesiastical, and cultural. Although the occasional friar or bishop appears elsewhere (in *Romeo and Juliet*, for instance, and several history plays), *Measure for Measure* is clearly set in a more explicitly Catholic milieu than any of Shakespeare's other plays. Indeed, he even increases the prominence of religious institutions as compared with his sources: his innovations include the detail of making the disguised ruler adopt the disguise specifically of a friar, and representing Isabella as an aspirant nun, whereas her counterparts in Cinthio and Whetstone, though equally virtuous, are clearly secular. I want to suggest that, even as the Reformation in England exacerbated the actual marginality of convents, it simultaneously increased their usefulness as fictitious spaces in which women's ambiguous relation to the central institutions of early modern society could be reimagined. Perhaps Isabella's status as a novice of the order of St Clare should be seen as an unusual reworking of the comic convention whereby a young woman's sexuality is placed under a prohibition or restriction that must be overcome before she can enter into the marriage that provides comedy with its happy ending. *The Merchant of Venice* provides a Shakespearian example. Portia may not choose her own husband but has to marry the man who successfully completes the riddling, fairy-tale task of choosing between three caskets set by her father: 'so', she complains, 'is the will of a living daughter curbed by the will of a dead father' (1.2.23–4).

Isabella too is the daughter of a dead father; the convent gives her the opportunity to attach herself to a new symbolic mother, and she readily embraces the distinctly patriarchal relationship offered by the Duke, the man she calls 'good father' (3.1.240). In feminist scholarship, female communities have sometimes been perceived as creating a space for women outside patriarchal domination. In *Measure for Measure*, though, the convent does not so much exceed the bounds of regulation, as construct an alternative space where regulation operates differently, to different ends, and under different authority. This control and restraint are precisely what Isabella finds attractive about the convent – perhaps, we might hypothesize, because of the contrast it poses to the laxity of Viennese society – as her opening exchange with the nun Francisca demonstrates:

ISABELLA And have you nuns no farther privileges?
NUN Are not these large enough?
ISABELLA Yes, truly. I speak not as desiring more,
    But rather wishing a more strict restraint
    Upon the sisterhood, the votarists of Saint Clare.

(1.4.1–5)

Though the Catholic Church, in Shakespeare's time as now, is undoubtedly a patriarchal organization, the play emphasizes the self-regulation of the female community, to which men appear irrelevant, except as visitors, when strict rules are imposed to control their access to the female social space of the convent (1.4.10–13). But, when Isabella leaves the convent to move through the public space of Vienna, she submits herself readily to the authority of the Friar.

Isabella's experience of social and theatrical space is one of extremes, from the strict enclosure of the convent, to wanderings through the city, including such insalubrious locations as the prison, and beyond its boundaries to Mariana's moated grange.

45

In contrast to that of Isabella, though, Mariana's experience is one of confinement and isolation. And the converse of women's liberty to move through the city was imaged by the frequently used metaphor, which ultimately derives from both classical and biblical sources, of the female body as a walled garden.[4] The sealed boundaries of the garden act as symbolic guarantors of the woman's chastity before and especially during marriage, on which such a high cultural value was placed. It is ironically appropriate, then, that although it is not actually staged, a walled garden is mentioned in *Measure for Measure* as the place proposed for Isabella's secret nocturnal meeting with Angelo:

> He hath a garden circummured with brick,
> Whose western side is with a vineyard backed;
> And to that vineyard is a plankèd gate,
> That makes his opening with this bigger key.
> This other doth command a little door
> Which from the vineyard to the garden leads.
> There have I made my promise
> Upon the heavy middle of the night
> To call upon him.

> (4.1.27–35)

In Shakespeare's London, such gardens were notorious as places of illicit sexual encounter, and in *The Anatomie of Abuses* in 1583 the moralist Philip Stubbes railed against them in terms that might have instructed Shakespeare on the sexual usefulness of walled gardens, so closely do they correspond to the passage just quoted:

> In the Feeldes and Suburbes of the Cities thei have Gardens, either palled, or walled round about very high, with their Harbers, and Bowers fit for the purpose.... And for that their Gardens are locked, some of them have three or fower keyes a peece, whereof one they keepe for themselves, the other their Paramours have to goe in before them.... And truly I thinke some of these places are little better then the Stewes and Brothell houses were in tymes past.[5]

According to Stubbes, then, these pleasure gardens were urban or suburban spaces, embodying a kind of restricted, enclosed 'green world' in the city.

In contrast, Mariana's grange appears solitary and secluded. Granges were usually farms attached to religious houses, and so it should perhaps be considered another institutional setting, like the convent where we first meet Isabella. It is the only place in the play where music can be heard, and the song 'Take, O take those lips away' provides a poignant commentary on Mariana's situation. Though Shakespeare's script requires Mariana to be the listener while a boy singer ventriloquizes her grief, in modern production it is often Mariana herself who sings. In the 1994 Cheek by Jowl production, Marianne Jean-Baptiste as an alcohol-sodden Mariana sang an extended version of the song in a bluesy style, tapping into the cultural stereotype of black women as victims, finding solace or outlet in drugs and music, in a way that achieved a powerful theatrical effect. However, the victim stereotype was only one facet of Jean-Baptiste's subtle and highly praised performance, counter-balanced, for instance, by the wildly cynical cackle she let out when the Duke brought on a nun to solve all her problems for her. Intriguingly, having a black actress play Mariana has become a frequent practice, and one that would bear scrutiny – black Isabellas are much more scarce, and it is worth asking oneself why this is, and what the theatrical meanings of such casting decisions might be.

Measure for Measure has often been thought to date from roughly the same period of Shakespeare's career as *Hamlet* and has a good deal in common with that play. In particular, Hamlet's cry to Ophelia 'Get thee to a nunnery' is ironically relevant; for the pun that is submerged in *Hamlet*, playing on the fact that 'nunnery' was a slang term for brothel, takes on a kind of three-dimensional theatricality in *Measure for Measure*, where for much of the play the brothel and the convent seem to provide women with their only real options. The poet Isabella Whitney, writing a few decades earlier than Shakespeare, creates a picture of a London milieu that is vividly evocative of the socially marginal world of brothels, alehouses, and other urban pleasures depicted in *Measure for Measure*:

> At Steelyard store of wines there be,
> Your dulled minds to glad,
> And handsome men that must not wed,
> Except they leave their trade.
> They oft shall seek for proper girls,

And some perhaps shall find
(That need compels or lucre lures)
To satisfy their mind.
And near the same, I houses leave,
For people to repair
To bathe themselves, so to prevent
Infection of the air.[6]

Whitney is unusual among English Renaissance writers in suggesting that women might be driven to prostitution by economic need, rather than sexual desire, though an awareness of the commercial underpinning of prostitution is evident in all of Shakespeare's treatments of the theme. More common is the connection that is repeatedly made in *Measure for Measure* between the brothel and the hothouse or bathhouse (where people went to sweat out the symptoms of sexual disease), commercialized sex and sexually transmitted disease. This same link was made by an investigation into the underworld of the London suburbs, the Wardmote Inquest of 1617, which refers to 'any hot-house, or sweating-house, for ease and health of men, to which be resorting or conversant any strumpets or women of evil fame or name, or if there be any hot-house, or sweating-house ordained for women, to the which is any common recourse of young men'.[7] Here, the hothouse has itself become a place of sexual misconduct. A 1603 proclamation that called for the pulling-down of houses in the suburbs of London as a precaution against the spread of the plague by 'dissolute and idle persons' shows how easily such ideas could be extended to embrace a whole district or subculture, and may be one of the factors underlying Mrs Overdone's lament that her house is 'custom-shrunk'.

The imagined, offstage space of the brothel has come to play an important role in critical analyses of sexual politics and social order in Duke Vincentio's Vienna. Despite the fascination of the play – and perhaps even more so, of the critics and those who have realized it in the theatre – with the idea of prostitution, and the more general commodification of sexuality of which it is a symptom, Shakespeare scripts no entrances or speeches for the women who work in Mrs Overdone's house. We see no prostitutes, just Pompey and Mrs Overdone, pimp and madam of the unseen hothouse, and a lone client, the hapless Froth.

Pompey does, though, draw our attention to the men who provide the demand for prostitution when he lists the brothel customers who have ended up in prison, remarking in comic amazement, 'I am as well-acquainted here as I was in our house of profession. One would think it were Mistress Overdone's own house, for here be many of her old customers' (4.3.1–4). The humour of this speech has not stood the test of time well, though it can provide the actor playing Pompey with the opportunity for a virtuoso comic 'turn'. In the 1981 National Theatre production set on an imaginary Caribbean island, for instance, Oscar James as Pompey was a carnivalesque figure who transformed this speech into a calypso – a form of improvised song, unique to the Caribbean, which is usually a vehicle of topical social commentary.

Pompey has a dramatic counterpart in the figure of Boult the Bawd in the late, collaboratively composed play *Pericles*. Though *Pericles* does include several scenes set in or on the threshold of a brothel, and we are introduced to the couple who keep it, here too prostitutes are absent from the stage. Instead Marina, sold to Boult by pirates, succeeds in transforming the brothel from a place of commodified, exploited sexuality and its attendant miseries (notably sexually transmitted disease, the subject of endless jokes in Renaissance comedy) into something akin to a temple, and its former customers into virtuous men, more inclined to 'hear the vestals sing' than to 'rutting' (19.7.9). The process dramatized here seems to be the reverse of the one by which Isabella inadvertently provokes Angelo's lust by her purity. And ironically, Marina recommends to Boult the very career change that is imposed on Pompey:

> Empty
> Old receptacles or common sew'rs of filth,
> Serve by indenture to the common hangman –
> Any of these are better yet than this.

> (*Pericles*, 19.199–203)

Some critical and theatrical treatments of the brothel problematically romanticize it as a female social space, as if a brothel only has anything to do with the prostitutes who work there, and not the men who buy their services. This tendency to omit the clients from scrutiny while objectifying the prostitute, in a way that is at once glamorizing and degrading, is by no means unique to Shakespeare scholars, but rather is a staple of cultural discourse on prostitution. Consider, for example, the remarkably fertile list of terms for prostitute that Jonathan Dollimore has found in Shakespeare's plays: bawd, strumpet, callet, courtezan, drab, harlot, punk, stale, public commoner, fitchew, flirt-gills, skains-mate, galled goose of Winchester, quean, Amazonian trull, housewife.[8] An equivalent list of slang names for men who pay prostitutes for sex would be short indeed. It is arguable that the profusion of nicknames for prostitutes is indicative of the extent to which female sexuality in the early modern period is prone to be commodified, and to be seen as potentially a matter of exchange between men. Pompey's 'strange pick-lock' (3.1.285), for example, presumably designed to enable him to pick the locks of chastity belts, represents female sexuality as a valuable commodity that must be kept locked up because women cannot be trusted to guard it themselves. This translates the lyrical image of female sexuality as a walled garden, mentioned earlier, into a mode at once more comic and more punitive. Such a perception of female sexuality is grounded in the fact that marriage in the early modern world was a property transaction as much as a matter of personal affection. Angelo's desertion of Mariana when her dowry was lost also demonstrates this.

The task of managing the lucrative business of sexual commodification in *Measure for Measure* lies in the hands of Pompey and Mrs Overdone – in Peter Brook's 1950 production, Pompey, when brought before the court in Act 2, Scene 1, seized the opportunity to extend the client base in lucrative new directions by handing out cards advertising Mrs Overdone's establishment. Like Mistress Quickly and Doll Tearsheet, the inn hostess and prostitute who appear in 1 and 2 *Henry IV*, Mrs Overdone is in many ways an appealing figure. This is established, for instance, by the fact that she is first introduced to us in the context of her sentimental attitude to Claudio, as she sighs to Lucio and his bantering friends that 'There's one yonder arrested and carried to prison was worth five thousand of you all' (1.2.58–60). For modern readers and audiences, she can be perceived as the voice of a pragmatic, positive evaluation of the pleasure and utility of human sexuality that is all too rare in the world of the play. Thus her assertion that 'within these three days his head [is] to be chopped off... for getting Madam Julietta with child' (1.2.67, 70–1) suggests both that Claudio's crime has, in effect, been to get caught, and that the punishment is a grotesquely brutal one, endorsing Lucio's later explanation to Isabella that Claudio is in prison

> For that which, if myself might be his judge,
> He should receive his punishment in thanks:
> He hath got his friend with child.

(1.4.27–9)

The feminist critic Jyotsna Singh places Mistress Overdone as a contestatory voice in the play, one who strives to tell a story about prostitution not as a moral evil, but as a socially, politically, and economically determined practice. Singh argues that 'her discourse of the commodification of female sexuality disrupts the dominant discourse of sexual morality with its strong biblical undertones',[9] and draws the classic feminist analogy between this commodification and that of marriage.

Mrs Overdone's lament about the falling-off of trade – 'Thus what with the war, what with the sweat, what with the gallows, and what with poverty, I am custom-shrunk' (1.2.80–2) – is often treated in the context of a topical approach to the play, which sees it as engaging with events and issues that were of immediate concern to the theatre audiences for whom it was written. Editing the play for the Arden Shakespeare in 1965, for example, Lever commented, 'Overdone's complaint links a number of factors operative in the winter of 1603–4: the continuance of the war with Spain; the plague in London; the treason trials and executions at Winchester in connection with the plots of Raleigh and others; the slackness of trade in the deserted capital.'[10] This accumulation of detail is persuasive; but this was certainly not the only year when disease, execution, and poverty might have caused Mrs Overdone to be 'custom-shrunk'. Rather than pinning her dismal remark down to a single set of topical references, it seems more useful to me to underline her perception of prostitution as an aspect of social existence that intertwines with other important aspects of city life. This understanding of prostitution is one that is developed throughout *Measure for Measure*, notably by the Duke. In the final scene, for example, still in his role as Friar, he admits with disgust that in Vienna 'I have seen corruption boil and bubble/ Till it o'errun the stew' (5.1.315–16). This word play combines the familiar domestic image of a cooking pot boiling over with the seventeenth-century use of 'stew' as a slang term for brothel, and seems to imply that the 'stew' is the source of all corruption in Vienna. But it is surely arguable that the reverse is true, and that corruption and social disorder in the city proceed from the Duke's confessed failure to rule adequately, as well as the hypocrisy and viciousness of his deputy, as Jonathan Dollimore proposed in his important account of the play: 'Prostitution and lechery are identified as the causes of crisis, yet we learn increasingly of a corruption more political than sexual....[T]he play discloses corruption to be an effect less of desire than of authority itself.'[11] The Duke would like to make Mrs Overdone and her colleagues take the blame for Viennese disorder, but he should perhaps be more concerned about the acuteness of their critical insights into the real causes of the city's problems. Though Mrs Overdone, for instance, is dismayed that all the 'houses of resort in the suburbs' (1.2.93–4) are to be pulled down, Pompey notes that the same fate would have befallen those in the city, were it not for metropolitan corruption: 'a wise burgher put in for them' (1.2.92). Pompey doubts the efficacy of the law against fornication because it seems to him to be enforceable only at a comically dystopian cost, entailing the depopulation of Vienna and consequent economic collapse:

POMPEY Does your worship mean to geld and splay all the youth of the city?
ESCALUS No, Pompey.
POMPEY Truly, sir, in my poor opinion they will to't then. If your worship will take order for the drabs and the knaves, you need not to fear the bawds.
ESCALUS There is pretty orders beginning, I can tell you; it is but heading and hanging.
POMPEY If you head and hang all that offend that way but for ten year together, you'll be glad to give out a commission for more heads. If this law hold in Vienna ten year, I'll rent the fairest house in it after three pence a bay; if you live to see this come to pass, say Pompey told you so.

(2.1.220–33)

In the closing decades of the twentieth century, several productions of *Measure for Measure* have given the role of Mrs Overdone considerable prominence, often interpreting it inventively, even provocatively. Caroline Blakiston, in the 1994 Royal Shakespeare Company production, was at once elegant and raddled, glamorous and seedy: seated in a wheelchair presumably inspired by Mrs Overdone's complaints about pains in her hips (symptomatic of sexually transmitted disease) she was beautifully dressed in a fur coat and satin underwear, but looked ill and unhappy, as if she had, to paraphrase Pompey, been worn out in the service. Strikingly different was Keith Hack's staging for the Royal Shakespeare Company some twenty years earlier, in which Dan Meaden offered a fabulously over-the-top rendition of Mrs Overdone as a grotesque drag queen, with a big Cupid's-bow mouth and a shock of ginger curls. I have already mentioned the play on words that in the seventeenth century made 'nunnery' a slang term for brothel: Meaden embodied this by doubling as Francesca the nun, changing costume and moving from one role to the other in full view of the audience.

The growth of scholarly interest in the meanings of the brothel in *Measure for Measure* has been matched by a tendency in productions of the play to bring the prostitutes onstage, even though no roles are allocated to them in Shakespeare's script. At her entrance in Act 1, Scene 2, for example, Mrs Overdone is often accompanied by a knot of disconsolate prostitutes, whose gestures and stances offer a choric accompaniment to her laments about the damage that the proclamation will do to trade. But the theatrical effects created by the staging of these prostitutes can run counter to the direction of critical analysis. In appropriating the commodification of sexuality for theatrical ends rather than critiquing it, they run the risk of reproducing stereotypical images of prostitutes. At Stratford in 1994, for example, Mrs Overdone was accompanied by a glum group of gum-chewing rent boys in leather, and tousle-haired women in leopard-print mini-skirts and fishnet stockings. Though they overcame their apathy long enough to launch a mini-riot against the forces of state oppression at the moment of Mrs Overdone's arrest in Act 3, Scene 1, this was an embarrassingly half-hearted and clichéd attempt to convey a sense of the brothel's seedy glamour and dangerous decadence.

More effective was the moment in the same production when Pompey brought on stage a very young girl, barely in her teens, whom he had recruited to the prostitutes' ranks. This, of course, was a piece of stage business that has no warrant in Shakespeare's text, but it was very powerful, serving both to complicate the audience's response to Pompey – generally presented as a highly sympathetic figure – and to demand that we think about the social and economic forces that drive women to prostitution. We might see it as creating a kind of theatrical counterpart to Mrs Overdone's lament about the social factors that are causing the demand for prostitutes to fall off, illustrating that the supply is similarly socially determined. At the same time, the priorities of contemporary criticism should not lead to a reinvention of *Measure for Measure* as a critique of the commodification of female sexuality: as jokily appropriate names like Mrs Overdone and Kate Keepdown suggest, ideas about prostitution are here employed very much for comic, theatrical purposes.

I have argued against the romanticization of the brothel as a female social space, and one man who is presented as being familiar with, even part of, the prostitutes' world, is Lucio. Socially and theatrically mobile, he mediates between the world of Pompey, Mrs Overdone, Kate Keepdown, and his own bastard child, and that of Claudio, Isabella, the Duke, and the other élite characters. His first appearance typifies this liminal, mobile function, since the innuendo-laden banter between him and the two anonymous gentlemen turns on issues that are central to the play's most serious concerns: grace, law, and the individual's relation to those powerful abstractions. Shortly afterwards, he is made a messenger from Claudio in prison, convicted of a sexual crime, to Isabella in the convent, who is about to take a vow of chastity. The list of dramatis personae in the 1623 Folio identifies Lucio as 'a fantastique', and in the Overburian characters, a series of brief, witty descriptions of stereotyped figures that achieved great popularity in the early seventeenth century, the description of 'A Phantastique: An Improvident Young Gallant' is comically reminiscent of Lucio: 'He accounts bashfulnesse the wickedest thing in the world; and therefore studies impudence. If all men were of his mind, all honesty would be out of fashion. . . . He is travelled, but to little purpose; only went over for a squirt, and come back againe, yet never the more mended in his conditions, 'cause he carried himselfe along with him.'[12] It cannot be denied that Lucio sometimes plays fast and loose with the truth, for instance in his exchanges with the Duke/Friar. Yet it does not seem quite fair to describe him as thoroughly dishonest. Lucio seems to represent an alternative set of values that cannot be reconciled with those that win out in the play, but that hold considerable appeal for readers and spectators. In this, and in the seductive opportunities that the role offers an actor, he is very much like Mercutio in *Romeo and Juliet*.

When Lucio brings Isabella the news that Claudio 'hath got his friend with child' (1.4.29), she soon realizes that this must be 'my cousin Juliet' (1.4.44). The relationship is not one of blood, though, but of choice: they are cousins 'Adoptedly, as schoolmaids change their names / By vain though apt affection' (1.4.46–7). This glimpse of long-established friendship between Isabella and Juliet recalls the touching evocations of friendship between young girls in plays such as *A Midsummer Night's Dream* and *The Two Noble Kinsmen*, and offers a rare opportunity in this play to see women relating to each other outside the framework of patriarchal institutions such as the brothel and convent, or beyond the manipulations of the Friar/Duke. But after this brief acknowledgment of Juliet, Isabella seems to forget her entirely. Indeed, except for the last sixty lines or so of the play, they are never even on stage together, and so there is no dramatic space where the relationship between them could be developed.

In the whole play, in fact, there are just two moments when women are on the stage without any men present: the brief conversation about the privileges and restraints attendant on convent life between Isabella and the nun Francisca at 1.4.1–5, and the appearance of Isabella and Mariana at 4.6.1–8. Ironically, this latter scene is entirely taken up with the women's discussion of the instructions given them by the man they know as Friar Lodowick, and even this conversation is interrupted by the arrival of his emissary, Friar Peter. Women are not only isolated from each other in Vienna, they are outnumbered by and subordinated to men. The staging of the final scene often brings out the implications of this forcefully: at Stratford in 1994, Isabella – dressed in a man's suit, yet with her femininity emphasized by her mop of curly blonde hair – and Mariana, clad head to toe in red chiffon, as if to incarnate the scarlet woman of sexist cliché, were lonely, vulnerable figures in front of a ring of some sixty male judges, professors, priests, and aristocrats. Having made their plea for Angelo's life, they huddled together as if for comfort, their fate in the hands of this crowd of men, threatened with prison and denounced as madwomen ('her wits I fear me are not firm', (5.1.33)), no better than prostitutes – 'she may be a punk, for many of them are neither maid, widow, nor wife', as Lucio charmlessly responds to the riddle of Mariana's identity (5.1.177–8). Reviewer Benedict Nightingale described, the 'long chortle of clubby male glee' that greeted Isabella's admission that she no longer had the right to name herself 'a maid' (5.1.21),[13] making painfully clear where power lay in Vienna, and how hard it would be for a woman to gain access to the justice Isabella demands.

In this chapter, I have focused on the sexual politics of social and theatrical space in Shakespeare's Vienna. The final scene's use of theatrical space reconstructs the social space of Vienna in ways that return us, with a difference, to the play's opening. There is an emphasis both on liminality and on the symbolic meaning of places in the insistence that the meeting occur at or near the gates, and in the reference to the 'consecrated fount/A league below the city' (4.3.94–5). If the Duke's departure from Vienna was discreet and private, his re-entry to the city is to be a thoroughly heralded and public affair. The main purpose of Act 4, Scene 5, beyond furthering the complex machinations needed to bring off the Duke's plots in the final scene, seems to be to create a sense of ceremonial surrounding his return to Vienna, as the arrival of Varrius to escort him into the city is accompanied by complex arrangements for his welcome. A general sense of bustle is dignified, even rendered triumphal, by the pseudo-classical names given to these attendants:

> Go call at Flavius' house,
> And tell him where I stay. Give the like notice
> To Valentius, Rowland, and to Crassus,
> And bid them bring the trumpets to the gate.

> (4.5.6–9)

This is extended, in the opening lines of the final scene, by the formal, mildly ceremonial quality of the greetings exchanged by the Duke, Angelo, and Escalus. In performance, this entrance is often seized as an opportunity to stage civic spectacle in ways that comment on the central concerns of the play. The Duke's apparent acknowledgement of Angelo's 'desert' (5.1.9–16) is fraught with dramatic irony; the speech concludes with an invitation to both Angelo and Escalus to join the triumphal procession on either side of the Duke (5.1.16–18): 'and good supporters are you', he says, imaging them as the heraldic supporters on either side of a shield. It is this formidable moment, in which the homosocial public sphere displays its apparent unity, that is so dramatically interrupted by Isabella's cry for justice. In the 1994 Royal Shakespeare Company production, Stella Gonet as Isabella had to confront a mass of uniformed men, visibly embodying the institutional powers of the patriarchy. It is striking, then, that Isabella's plea is phrased in a way that immediately draws attention to her compromised status as a woman:

> Justice, O royal Duke! Vail your regard
> Upon a wronged – I would fain have said, a maid.

> (5.1.20–1)

From the safely enclosed, feminized space of the convent, through the strange territories of the prison, Mariana's grange, and the Viennese streets, Isabella's journey ends here, at the heart of Vienna's power structures. The outcome of her encounter with the city's institutions will be the subject of the final chapter.

4

Tortured into a Comedy

Measure for Measure, along with some other Shakespeare plays that date from the first few years of the seventeenth century, is often referred to as a 'problem play': *All's Well That Ends Well* and *Troilus and Cressida* are the other plays most often included in this curious category. At times, this designation seems to indicate little more than a desire to tidy away Shakespeare's plays into neatly classified and labelled boxes – a desire that is frustrated by the diversity of the plays, and by the complex and inventive ways in which Shakespeare experimented with dramatic genre. But it is also a label that can be very revealing about changing attitudes to this strange and fascinating play, and in particular about the shifts in readers' and audiences' responses to its handling of the central, controversial issues of power, justice, sexuality, and the relation between religious principle and social practice.

The term 'problem play' is a modern one, which would have been entirely unfamiliar to Shakespeare, yet a century after it was first applied to *Measure for Measure* and a few other plays it has become so familiar that it is taken for granted. It may therefore be useful to look at it afresh, setting it in historical context in order to indicate what it means and how it came into use. In the mid-twentieth century, there was a widespread notion that Shakespeare wrote the so-called problem plays during a period of his life when he was experiencing some kind of personal turmoil, which found expression in the bitter, misanthropic nature of his work. More often, though, the 'problem' has been located in the structure or content of the plays themselves. The plays were first described in this way by the scholar Frederick S. Boas in 1896:

Fig. 7. Sarah Siddons, in a celebrated romantic interpretation of Isabella.

Stephen Macmillan

Fig. 8. Juliet Stevenson, one of the finest recent Isabellas, with Daniel Massey as the Duke in the 1983 RSC production directed by Adrian Noble.

throughout these plays we move along dim untrodden paths, and at the close our feeling is neither of simple joy nor pain; we are excited, fascinated, perplexed, for the issues raised preclude a completely satisfactory outcome....Dramas so singular in theme and temper cannot be strictly called comedies or tragedies. We may therefore borrow a convenient phrase from the theater of today and class them together as Shakspere's [sic] problem-plays.[1]

Boas did not, therefore, invent the term, which was already in use to describe the plays of writers such as Ibsen and Shaw, whose dramas treated complex social problems of the time, often in a mode that mingled the tragic and comic and left endings open and unresolved. Indeed, in the late nineteenth century, reviews of *Measure for Measure* and of contemporary 'problem plays' often perceive them in strikingly similar terms. Discussing a New York production directed by Helena Modjeska (who also played Isabella) in 1896, just at the turn of the century in which the play was to achieve new popularity and prominence, one reviewer complained that her efforts to eliminate the play's 'nastiness' were futile, 'for the trouble is radical'; she 'covered the cesspool...but it is there,' nevertheless, breeding disease and distorting minds'.[2] Similarly, Ibsen and the other authors of the nineteenth-century 'problem plays' who influenced Boas were accused of descending into the gutter and wallowing in psychological filth.

In both *Measure for Measure* and its late-Victorian counterparts, the exploration of these social issues is often organized around questions of sexuality and marriage. The problem plays of Ibsen and his contemporaries are frequently concerned with the processes by which past sexual transgressions, hitherto kept secret, become known and therefore subject to the moral strictures and disciplinary powers of the public realm. Heroines, in particular, find their present and future under threat because of their sexual past: Ibsen's *Hedda Gabler* is a good example of this. *Measure for Measure* has a complicated and mixed relation to this issue, in ways that reveal the interweaving of sexuality, morality, and power. On the one hand, it shows the traumatic consequences of extending the legal surveillance of people's behaviour into what we might consider the private realm of sexuality; on the other, it shows how hard it can be to bring sexual wrongdoing into the light and have it acknowledged and believed. Thus, Claudio and Juliet's main fault seems to be letting the premature consummation of their marriage be betrayed by the corporal sign of Juliet's pregnancy: as Lucio says, Claudio is to be executed because 'He hath got his friend with child' (1.4.29). On the other hand, Angelo's warning to Isabella that no one will believe her accusations against a man of his status and reputation seems incontrovertible:

> ISABELLA Sign me a present pardon for my brother,
> Or with an outstretched throat I'll tell the world aloud
> What man thou art.
> ANGELO   Who will believe thee, Isabel?
> My unsoiled name, the austereness of my life,
> My vouch against you, and my place i'the state,
> Will so your accusation overweigh
> That you shall stifle in your own report
> And smell of calumny.

(2.4.152–9)

The unusual length of line 153 mimics Isabella's straining, in the final scene, to project her voice into an arena where – despite the apparent fulfilment of Angelo's warning that she will be disbelieved and humiliated – her cry for justice can ultimately be heard. Similarly, the irreconcilable accounts that Angelo and Mariana offer of the history of their relationship show the difficulty of establishing the truth about the sexual past. Angelo draws on dominant ideologies of sexuality and courtship to make his case, claiming that Mariana's dowry was inadequate ('her promised proportions/Came short of composition' (5.1.217–18)) and that her behaviour did not conform to his expectations of his bride: 'her reputation was disvalued/In levity' (5.1.219–20). Mariana has to rely on 'words from breath' (5.1.223), words that 'make up vows' (5.1.226). But her words are not acceptable to this impromptu court, and it is only when the Duke emerges from his disguise to endorse her story that she is believed.

Reviewing the history of critical and theatrical responses to *Measure for Measure*, it often seems that all the problems posed by the play coalesce in the extraordinary dramatic, moral, and social tensions engendered in its long, demanding final scene. Within two hundred lines of the ending of the play, *Measure for Measure* seems to be set on a course for tragedy, though admittedly the tragic mood is repeatedly punctured by Lucio's lewd and witty commentary. Only in the last hundred lines or so is the happy ending of comedy secured, with the arrangement of multiple marriages, and the return to the stage of Claudio as if from beyond the grave. What is repeatedly emphasized in attempts to make sense of *Measure for Measure*'s problematic generic status is this mixed, uneven quality. One way of tackling this has been to argue that the play belongs to the specifically mixed genre of tragicomedy, which at the beginning of the seventeenth century was a new, avant-garde form that was to enjoy considerable popularity in the succeeding decades. Towards the end of his career, Shakespeare collaborated on several plays with John Fletcher, a successful practitioner of tragicomedy. Fletcher offered an intriguing definition of tragicomedy, portraying it not as an independent genre in its own right, so much as a failure to conform to generic requirements: 'it wants deaths, which is enough to make it no tragedy, yet brings some near it, which is enough to make it no comedy.'[3] Conventionally, the avoidance of deaths and the guarantee of a happy ending provide tragicomic drama with satisfactory closure. What make *Measure for Measure* different from tragicomedy, therefore, and uniquely problematic, are the discomfort and uncertainty that the ostensibly happy ending generates.

In remarking of *Measure for Measure*, 'it is a comedy of the flesh and a tragedy of the soul'[4] the nineteenth-century American commentator Edward Arlington Robinson oddly prefigured another way of thinking about the mixed, multifaceted nature of *Measure for Measure*, an approach to the play that was to be offered by the celebrated theatre director Peter Brook. His 1950 production with the Royal Shakespeare Company at Stratford has been described as the single event that did most to establish the play as a standard of the modern Shakespearian repertoire. Some twenty years later, Brook returned to *Measure for Measure* in his influential book on theatre, *The Empty Space*. Brook sketches out an overarching theory of theatre, which has two key facets: the Holy and the Rough. Holy Theatre is the 'Theatre of the Invisible – Made – Visible',[5] a sacred ritual that makes possible a glimpse of the eternal in the everyday. Rough Theatre embodies the popular in all its multifaceted, grotesque, satirical directness. Brook argues that in *Measure for Measure* these two elements coexist almost schematically, and are vitally inter-dependent: the 'absolutely convincing roughness and dirt' of the 'disgusting, stinking world of medieval Vienna' give Isabella's plea for grace more meaning than it would have in 'lyrical comedy's never-never land'. The press release for the 1950 production said that the designs – for which Brook was also responsible – drew on the work of the artists Brueghel and Bosch to reflect 'the cruelty, vice and squalor of medieval Vienna'. But records of the staging and Brook's discussion of the play in *The Empty Space* testify to an understanding of this aspect of *Measure for Measure* that is reminiscent of the notion of the grotesque or carnivalesque found in the work of Mikhail Bakhtin. By means of a study of festivity in medieval Europe, Bakhtin traces the cultural uses of release – even if constrained and temporary – from the rules and conventions that govern everyday life, identifying the grotesque as a source of liberatory or critical energies. Brook takes up a similar stance in relation to *Measure for Measure*, arguing that 'when so much of the play is religious in thought, the loud humour of the brothel is important as a device, because it is alienating and human-izing.'[6] The idea that particular dramatic strategies can be used to alienate – roughly, to distance and challenge – the audience is derived from the work of Bertolt Brecht, who, as we have already seen, brought a distinctive, politicized attitude to bear on *Measure for Measure* in the 1930s. What the notion of alienation implies here is that the rough world of the prison and the streets of Vienna enable the audience to adopt a critical stance in relation to the religious world view that informs the behaviour of the central characters. Brook argues that in *Measure for Measure* the rough world expresses itself in prose, the holy in verse, and that these two regions of the play require different approaches in staging. For him, therefore, the vitality and significance of the play lie in Shakespeare's 'ever-shifting devices': 'If we follow the movement in *Measure for Measure* between the Rough and the Holy we will discover a play about justice, mercy, honesty, forgiveness, virtue, virginity, sex and death: kaleidoscopically one section of the play mirrors the other, it is in accepting the prism as a whole that its meanings emerge.'[7] Brook sees this mobility and multiplicity as the distinctive features of Shakespeare's plays in general, but as particularly central to *Measure for Measure*. In his account, therefore, *Measure for Measure* moves from being a marginal and problematic Shakespearian play, to one that can almost be taken as representative of Shakespeare's whole approach to theatre.

Though Brook's influence has been considerable, it is not solely due to him that in Europe and North America in the late twentieth century *Measure for Measure* has become one of the most frequently staged of Shakespeare's plays. However, its popularity was not always so assured, and its chequered fortunes on the stage are very instructive about changing perceptions of its 'problems'. The Revels Accounts, which document performances at the Jacobean court, note that a play by 'Shaxberd' called '*Mesur for Mesur*' was performed, probably for the first time, in the principal London court theatre, the Banqueting Hall in Whitehall on St Stephen's Night (26 December) 1604. It is hard to know what to make of these facts. Though the date obviously indicates that the performance formed part of the extended period of Christmas festivities, and it is widely accepted by scholars that the audience included King James, who had been on the throne of England and Wales for just a few months at this point, these disparate scraps of information cannot furnish a clear sense of how this first audience might have responded to the play. What we do know is that there is no further record of any performances of *Measure for Measure* in London before the theatres closed in 1642. We should, though, bear in mind the possibility that there were other performances, in London or when the players were on tour in other parts of the country, and that the play was more popular than this apparent absence from the stage would suggest.

This contention is supported by the fact that it was one of the first of Shakespeare's plays to be performed when the theatres reopened in 1660 – albeit in thoroughly rearranged form. Sir William Davenant, one of the most influential figures in the London theatre of the 1660s, adapted several of Shakespeare's plays. He hit on the ingenious idea of combining *Measure for Measure* with *Much Ado about Nothing*, throwing in an armed revolution, and closing the play (rechristened *The Law against Lovers*) by marrying off Isabella to Angelo while the Duke retires to a monastery. Prim and sentimental in comparison with Shakespeare's play, Davenant's adaptation seeks to make *Measure for Measure* into a more straightforwardly comic piece, softening its rough edges in accordance with Restoration taste. Similarly, in 1700, Charles Gildon decided that, as the basis of a night's entertainment, *Measure for Measure* would be improved by being interwoven with Purcell's 1689 opera *Dido and Aeneas*: though separately both these works are quite wonderful, the combination does no favours to either of them.

The fact that dramatists of this period saw Shakespeare's plays as a kind of quarry from which attractive but rough-hewn lumps of dramatic material could be mined and reworked to make them more aesthetically pleasing tells us a good deal about the changes that his reputation and status have undergone over the centuries. The adaptations of Davenant and Gildon reveal a sense that, while *Measure for Measure* has potential, it is commercially unsatisfactory because it fails to conform to the tastes of the age, and this is what they seek to rectify. Later in the eighteenth century, though, a sense that there was something more deeply troubling about the play began to crystallize. This perception was vividly articulated by Charlotte Lennox, a prolific writer across a range of fictional and non-fictional forms, who is now less well known than she deserves to be. With the three volumes of her *Shakespear Illustrated*, published in 1753–4, Lennox pioneered the source-study of Shakespeare's plays, translating 'the Novels and Histories on which the Plays of Shakespear are founded', and offering critical comment on the transformations Shakespeare wrought on his material.[8] Lennox valued Shakespeare's originality, and argued that what he did with his sources was more significant than the eventful histories he found in them: 'a very small Part of the Reputation of this mighty Genius depends upon the naked Plot, or Story of his Plays.'[9] As we have seen, the densely detailed theatrical world of *Measure for Measure* is shaped out of a wide range of cultural materials, from the Bible to contemporary thinking about prisons, and modern scholarship takes account of this. Charlotte Lennox's project was more narrowly defined, and she concentrated on exploring the relevance to *Measure for Measure* of Novella 5 of Decade 8 of the Italian writer Giraldi Cinthio's *Hecatommithi* (1565).

Like Chaucer's *Canterbury Tales*, the *Hecatommithi* is a compendium of stories supposedly told by a group of travellers to beguile the duller moments of their journey (another of the tales provided Shakespeare with the basic situation and story for *Othello*). The story that underlies *Measure for Measure* concerns a young man called Vico, Claudio's counterpart, whose beautiful and virtuous sister Epitia, lacking a puppet-master Duke to stage a bed-trick for her, is obliged to submit to the hypocritical Iuriste, an Angelo-like figure acting as deputy for the absent Emperor Maximian. Piratical substitutes being unavailable in Cinthio's narrative, Vico is executed, to the horror and rage of his sister. On the Emperor's return, Epitia, no less eloquent than Isabella and more readily believed, reveals the wrong that has been done to her and her brother. Appalled, the Emperor orders Iuriste to make amends for his two crimes, by marrying Epitia, and then submitting to execution. Epitia begs for the life of her newly-acquired husband to be spared; moved by her goodness, Maximian agrees, and the conclusion of the novella assures us that they will enjoy a long and happy marriage.

Though Charlotte Lennox was in general an enthusiast for Shakespeare, she was thoroughly underwhelmed by his handling of this story in *Measure for Measure*. She shared with many of her literary contemporaries a commitment to the moral function of art, and like other readers – notably Samuel Johnson, one of the era's most celebrated commentators on Shakespeare – she found the endings of both Cinthio's tale and Shakespeare's play emotionally frustrating and morally unsatisfactory:

> That *Shakespear* made a wrong Choice of his Subject, since he was resolved to torture it into a Comedy, appears by the low Contrivance, absurd Intrigue, and Improbable Incident, he was obliged to introduce, in order to bring about three or four Weddings, instead of one good Beheading, which was the Consequence naturally expected.... This play therefore being absolutely defective in a due Distribution of Rewards and Punishments; *Measure for Measure* ought not to be in the Title, since Justice is not the Virtue it inculcates...[10]

In Lennox's attack, moral concerns are intertwined with a strong sense of the requirements of genre, which are not met by the ending of this play. Though the terms in which she makes this charge are very much of her time, the basic sentiment has been shared by many subsequent audiences and readers. I have already mentioned how close the ending of the play comes to tragedy; I want now to suggest that the final scene has echoes in particular of the subgenre of revenge tragedy, extremely popular at the turn of the seventeenth century, and a form in which Shakespeare showed himself to be adept with plays such as *Titus Andronicus* and *Hamlet*. In revenge tragedy, a mourner finds it impossible to get redress for the murder of a loved one through the normal channels of justice, usually because these have been corrupted and have fallen into the hands of the murderer or their allies. Thus the revenger is driven to seek justice by alternative means, often being forced to take the law into his or her own hands: Shakespeare's contemporary Bacon famously described revenge as a 'kind of wild justice'. In this case, Isabella holds Angelo responsible for the judicial murder of Claudio, and in phrasing that echoes one of the most successful revenge dramas, *The Spanish Tragedy*, directs her call for redress – 'Justice, O royal Duke! . . . justice, justice, justice, justice!' (5.1.20, 25) – to a source of authority in which she still trusts. But, as I noted in the previous chapter, this impassioned plea erupts into a formal, ceremonial moment as the returned Duke invites Escalus and Angelo to walk beside him in a public demonstration of the masculine unity of those who rule Vienna. And the dramatic impact of the moment underlines the revenger's exclusion from the circuits of power and entitlement. To place Isabella and her call for justice, which resonates through the final scene (the word is used eleven times) within the theatrical revenge tradition sharpens the focus of the contest between the law that demands 'measure for measure' in the form of appropriate retribution, and the more merciful law which requires its subjects to judge as they would be judged, to measure as they would be measured. The Duke pretends to assume that Angelo would have operated according to this latter principle: 'If he had so offended / He would have weighed thy brother by himself, / And not have cut him off' (5.1.110–12). But it is Isabella who puts it into practice, when she lays aside the revenger's obligation and joins Mariana in pleading for Angelo's life. Playing Isabella in Peter Brook's 1950 production, Barbara Jefford was instructed to pause at this point for as long as she thought the audience could bear: legend has it that she sometimes remained speechless and immobile for over a minute, producing an extraordinarily tense demonstration of the theatrical power of silence.

Though they do not receive an immediate answer, Angelo is saved and Isabella's generosity rewarded a few moments later when Claudio is produced by the Provost. The siblings' reunion is another of the play's many eloquent silences, in which bodily performance must fill in for absent speech, though its intensity is indicated by the Duke's breaking-off of his ineptly timed proposal to Isabella:

> If he be like your brother, for his sake
> Is he pardoned, and for your lovely sake,
> Give me your hand and say you will be mine,
> He is my brother too – but fitter time for that.

>   (5.1.489–92)

This leads us, of course, to *Measure for Measure*'s most famous and problematic silence, that with which Isabella greets the Duke's reiterated proposal in the closing moments of the play. We cannot know how this fraught moment would have been played by Shakespeare's company. In modern productions, actors and directors have to decide whether Isabella's unscripted response to the Duke's proposal of marriage should be a positive or negative one, and how this should be indicated in gesture or movement. The actress Juliet Stevenson, who played Isabella to considerable acclaim with the Royal Shakespeare Company in 1983, suggests that, though this question must always be addressed in production, a definitive answer to it can never be achieved: 'there isn't a fixed end to the play. The *script* ends. The words run out. But the *ending* – that's something that has to be renegotiated every performance.'[11]

As Juliet Stevenson's comment shows, performance history is important because, where discussion in the classroom, the scholarly journal, or among readers can examine the supposedly problematic aspects of the play from all angles and yet leave them unresolved, in the theatre decisions about how to solve these problems – if only in the most provisional and temporary way – have to be taken time after time. Some Isabellas flatly refuse the Duke, and this can provide the play with a powerful ending, although one that seems to work against the grain of its generic movement towards closure in marriage. In contrast, Stevenson herself succeeded, most unusually, in demonstrating the growth of love between Isabella and the Duke throughout the play, and so her considered, heartfelt acceptance of his proposal was no surprise. Two years earlier, in the National's Caribbean production, Yvette Harris's lithe, confident Isabella had also accepted her Duke gladly, appearing honoured by his proposal. Darker, more troubled readings have been offered: Robin Phillips's Freudian staging in Canada in 1975 depicted an Isabella whose flight from sexual desire was defeated by the Duke's proposal, but who expressed her disillusionment and distress at the sexism of the culture that had ensnared her by violently ripping off the headdress of her white religious habit. More recently, Stella Gonet's Isabella brought out what one reviewer called the 'grim farce' of the play's uneasy, unstable conclusion by first slapping and then embracing the Duke, finally collapsing in tears. Isabella's significant silence holds open a space at the end of *Measure for Measure* that criticism and performance will always be driven to fill, but can never succeed in closing.

Notes

INTRODUCTION

1. *Kaleidoscope*, 18 May 1994. Cited from a transcript in the Cheek by Jowl archives. I am very grateful to the company for permitting me to use this material.
2. Michael Jamieson, 'The Problem Plays, 1920–1970: A Retrospect', *Shakespeare Survey*, 25 (1972), 1.
3. G. Wilson Knight, '*Measure for Measure* and the Gospels', in *The Wheel of Fire* (London: Oxford University Press, 1930), 79–80.

CHAPTER 1. OUR CITY'S INSTITUTIONS

1. See, e.g., Christopher Pye, *The Regal Phantasm: Shakespeare and the Politics of Spectacle* (London: Methuen, 1990), and Leonard Tennenhouse, *Power on Display: The Politics of Shakespeare's Genres* (London: Methuen, 1986).
2. Quoted in J. E. Neale, *Elizabeth I and her Parliaments* (London: Cape, 1953), 119.
3. *The Basilicon Doron of King James VI*, ed. James Craigie (Edinburgh: Scottish Text Society, 1944), 12.
4. Frank Whigham, 'Flattering Courtly Desire', in David L. Smith, Richard Strier, and David Bevington (eds.), *The Theatrical City: Culture, Theatre and Politics in London, 1576–1649* (Cambridge: Cambridge University Press, 1995), 139.
5. Jonathan Goldberg, *James I and the Politics of Literature* (Baltimore: Johns Hopkins University Press, 1983), 232.
6. Jacques Lezra, 'Pirating Reading: The Appearance of History in *Measure for Measure*', *ELH* 56/2 (1989), 261.
7. Jonathan Dollimore, 'Transgression and Surveillance in *Measure for Measure*', in Jonathan Dollimore and Alan Sinfield (eds.), *Political Shakespeare* (2nd edn.; Manchester: Manchester University Press, 1994), 81.

8. Richard Wilson, 'Prince of Darkness: Foucault's Shakespeare', in Nigel Wood (ed.), *Measure for Measure* (Buckingham: Open University Press, 1996), 176.
9. Pieter Spierenburg, 'The Body and the State: Early Modern Europe', in Norval Morris and David J. Rothman (eds.), *The Oxford History of the Prison: The Practice of Punishment in Western Society* (New York: Oxford University Press, 1995), 49–77.
10. *Report of the Charity Commissioners*, 1840, quoted in Wilson, 'Prince of Darkness', 141.
11. This account draws on A. L. Beier, *Masterless Men: The Vagrancy Problem in England, 1560–1640* (London, 1985); the quotations from Coke and other contemporary documents relating to prisons can also be found there.
12. Martha Widmayer, 'Mistress Overdone's House', in David G. Allen and Robert A. White (eds.), *Subjects on the World's Stage* (Newark, NJ: University of Delaware Press, 1995), 181–99.

CHAPTER 2. THE SCENE VIENNA

1. Leah Marcus, *Puzzling Shakespeare: Local Reading and its Discontents* (Berkeley and Los Angeles: University of California Press, 1988), 162.
2. Ibid. 197.
3. Louis Montrose, *The Purpose of Playing: Shakespeare and the Cultural Politics of the Elizabethan Theatre* (Chicago: Chicago University Press, 1996), 177.
4. See the revised and updated edition of E. A. J. Honigmann, *Shakespeare: The Lost Years* (Manchester: Manchester University Press, 1998).
5. Quoted in Meredith Anne Skura, *The Literary Use of the Psychoanalytic Process* (New Haven, Conn.: Yale University Press, 1981), 3.
6. Harriett Hawkins, *Measure for Measure* (Brighton: Harvester, 1987), 35.
7. Carolyn E. Brown, 'Erotic Religious Flagellation and Shakespeare's Measure for Measure', *English Literary Renaissance*, 16 (1986), 150.
8. Ibid. 140.
9. Ibid. 164.
10. Juliet Stevenson, quoted in Carol Rutter, *Clamorous Voices: Shakespeare's Women Today* (London: Women's Press, 1988), 43, 46, 49.
11. Ibid. 42, 43.
12. Paola Dionisotti, quoted in ibid. 39.
13. Janet Adelman, *Suffocating Mothers: Fantasies of Maternal Origin in Shakespeare's Plays* (London: Routledge, 1992), 90.

14. Michael Billington, review of *Measure for Measure*, in *The Guardian*, 20 June 1994.
15. Katherine Eisaman Maus, *Inwardness and Theater in the English Renaissance* (Chicago: Chicago University Press, 1995), 171.
16. Angela Carter (ed.), *The Virago Book of Fairy Tales* (London: Virago, 1990).
17. Jacqueline Rose, 'Sexuality in the Reading of Shakespeare: *Hamlet* and *Measure for Measure*', in John Drakakis (ed.), *Alternative Shakespeares* (London: Methuen, 1985), 95.
18. Ibid. 105.
19. G. Wilson Knight, '*Measure for Measure* and the Gospels', in *The Wheel of Fire* (London: Oxford University Press, 1930), 93.

CHAPTER 3.   HOUSES IN THE SUBURBS

1. Steven Mullaney, *The Place of the Stage: License, Play and Power in Renaissance England* (Chicago: Chicago University Press, 1988), 9.
2. Sara Mendelson and Patricia Crawford, *Women in Early Modern England 1550–1720* (Oxford: Clarendon Press, 1998), provides an excellent starting point for an exploration of this scholarship.
3. For a sampling of a wide range of attitudes to women's presence in theatre audiences, see S. P. Cerasano and Marion Wynne-Davies (eds.), *Renaissance Drama by Women: Texts and Documents* (London: Routledge, 1994), 161–7.
4. For a detailed discussion of this trope, see Peter Stallybrass, 'Patriarchal Territories: The Body Enclosed', in Margaret W. Ferguson, Maureen Quilligan, and Nancy Vickers (eds.), *Rewriting the Renaissance: Discourses of Sexual Difference in Early Modern Europe* (Chicago: Chicago University Press, 1986), 123–42.
5. Philip Stubbes, *The Anatomie of Abuses* (London, 1583), 48–9.
6. *The Will and Testament of Isabella Whitney* (1573), quoted in Lawrence Manley (ed.), *London in the Age of Shakespeare: An Anthology* (London: Croom Helm, 1986).
7. Quoted in ibid.
8. Jonathan Dollimore, 'Shakespeare Understudies: The Sodomite, the Prostitute, the Transvestite and their Critics', in Jonathan Dollimore and Alan Sinfield (eds.), *Political Shakespeare* (2nd edn.; Manchester: Manchester University Press, 1994), 136.
9. Jyotsna Singh, 'The Interventions of History', in Dympna Callaghan, Lorraine Helms, and Jyotsna Singh, *The Weyward Sisters: Shakespeare and Feminist Politics* (Oxford: Blackwell, 1994), 45.
10. J. M. Lever, Introduction, in Lever (ed.), *Measure for Measure* (Arden Shakespeare, 2nd ser.; London, 1965), p. xxxii.

11. Jonathan Dollimore, 'Transgression and Surveillance in *Measure for Measure*', in Jonathan Dollimore and Alan Sinfield (eds.), *Political Shakespeare* (2nd edn.; Manchester: Manchester University Press, 1994), 73.
12. Sir Thomas Overbury, *Characters* (London, 1613), 124–5.
13. Benedict Nightingale, *The Times*, 22 Oct. 1994.

CHAPTER 4. TORTURED INTO A COMEDY

1. Frederick S. Boas, *Shakspere and his Predecessors* (London: John Murray, 1896), 345.
2. Atherton Brownell, 'Rambles in Stageland', *The Bostonian* (Feb. 1896), cited in *Shakespearean Criticism*, 23 (1994), 281.
3. John Fletcher, quoted in Mark Eccles (ed.), *Measure for Measure* (New Variorum Edition of Shakespeare's Works; New York, 1980), 417.
4. Edward Arlington Robinson, quoted in ibid. 398.
5. Peter Brook, *The Empty Space* (Harmondsworth: Penguin, 1968), 42.
6. Ibid. 88.
7. Ibid. 89.
8. I draw here on the brief critical account of Lennox and the extracts from her work in Ann Thompson and Sasha Roberts (eds.), *Women Reading Shakespeare, 1660–1900* (Manchester: Manchester University Press, 1997), 15–21.
9. Ibid. 19.
10. Ibid. 16–18.
11. Juliet Stevenson, quoted in Carol Rutter, *Clamorous Voices: Shakespeare's Women Today* (London: Women's Press, 1988), 52.

Select Bibliography

OTHER EDITIONS OF *MEASURE FOR MEASURE*

Bawcutt, N. W., Oxford World's Classics (Oxford: Oxford University Press, 1991). Interesting account of stage history in the Introduction; annotation aimed mainly at clearing up difficulties of comprehension.

Eccles, Mark, New Variorum Edition of Shakespeare's Works (New York: Modern Language Association, 1980). Embeds the text in a detailed reception history; a useful resource.

Gibbons, Brian, New Cambridge Shakespeare (Cambridge: Cambridge University Press, 1991). Like the Oxford edition, has a good sense of the play's theatricality.

Ioppolo, Grace, Shakespeare Originals (Hemel Hempstead: Harvester, 1995). A reprint of the 1623 Folio with minimal editorial materials.

Lever, J. M., Arden Shakespeare (2nd ser.; London: Methuen, 1965). Still the best edition: the Introduction is itself an important contribution to the critical debate on *Measure for Measure*.

Nosworthy, J. M., New Penguin Shakespeare (Harmondsworth: Penguin, 1969). Portable and inexpensive, but perhaps the least substantial of the single-volume editions.

CRITICAL WORKS

Adelman, Janet, *Suffocating Mothers: Fantasies of Maternal Origin in Shakespeare's Plays* (London: Routledge, 1992). Reading *Measure for Measure* alongside *All's Well that Ends Well*, Adelman takes a psychoanalytic feminist approach to the plays' engagement with anxieties about maternity and marriage.

Battenhouse, Roy, '*Measure for Measure* and the Christian Doctrine of the Atonement', *PMLA* (*Publications of the Modern Language Association*) (1946). One of the most influential of explicitly

Christian critics of Shakespeare develops a reading of the play as a religious allegory.

Bennett, Josephine, *'Measure for Measure' as Royal Entertainment* (New York: Columbia University Press, 1966). Detailed topical reading, emphasizing the play's connections to Jacobean court culture.

Brook, Peter, *The Empty Space* (Harmondsworth: Penguin, 1968). An inspiring, idiosyncratic vision of the play from a theatre director who did much to reinstate *Measure for Measure* in the Shakespearian repertoire.

Bullough, Geoffrey, *Narrative and Dramatic Sources of Shakespeare*, ii. *Comedies 1597–1603* (London: Routledge & Kegan Paul, 1957). Useful extracts from Shakespeare's main sources.

Dollimore, Jonathan, 'Transgression and Surveillance in *Measure for Measure*', in Jonathan Dollimore and Alan Sinfield (eds.), *Political Shakespeare* (2nd edn.; Manchester: Manchester University Press, 1994), 72-87.

—— 'Shakespeare Understudies: The Sodomite, the Prostitute, the Transvestite and their Critics', in Dollimore and Sinfield (eds.), *Political Shakespeare*, 129–52. Two influential essays taking an essentially Foucauldian approach to the play's staging of discipline and transgression.

Gless, Darryl J., *'Measure for Measure', the Law, and the Convent* (Princeton: Princeton University Press, 1979). A meticulously documented study of the play's relation to contemporary discourses of law and religion.

Goldberg, Jonathan, *James I and the Politics of Literature* (Baltimore: Johns Hopkins University Press, 1983). A new historicist study that reconfigures the traditional critical identification of the Duke with James I to investigate the theatrical exercise of power in Jacobean London.

Hawkins, Harriett, *Measure for Measure* (Brighton: Harvester, 1987). Finds contradiction and controversy to be the source of *Measure for Measure*'s continued vigour as well as its status as a problem play.

Knight, G. Wilson, *'Measure for Measure* and the Gospels', in *The Wheel of Fire* (London: Oxford University Press, 1930), 73–96. Initiated a tendency to interpret *Measure for Measure* as a Christian allegory that dominated criticism in the mid-twentieth century.

Knights, L. C., 'The Ambiguity of *Measure for Measure*', *Scrutiny*, 10/2 (1942), 222–33; repr. in C. K. Stead (ed.), *Shakespeare, 'Measure for Measure': A Casebook* (Basingstoke: Macmillan, 1971), 138–51. Locating 'the sex instinct' at the heart of the play, Knights finds it to be an ambiguous work that fails to resolve the theatrical and moral problems it lays bare.

Lascelles, Mary, *Shakespeare's 'Measure for Measure'* (London: Athlone Press, 1953). Anticipating Hawkins, Lascelles offers a reading of the play that finds greatness in its unevenness, integrity in its complexity.

Leavis, F. R., 'The Greatness of *Measure for Measure'*, *Scrutiny*, 10/3 (1942), 234–47. Responding to Knights, Leavis asserted that the play was complex without being ambiguous, and firmly Christian in outlook.

McLuskie, Kathleen, 'The Patriarchal Bard: Feminist Criticism and Shakespeare: *King Lear* and *Measure for Measure'*, in Jonathan Dollimore and Alan Sinfield (eds.), *Political Shakespeare* (2nd edn.; Manchester: Manchester University Press, 1994, 88–108). An agenda-setting essay, which offers a materialist feminist reading of the play and argues that feminist criticism of *Measure for Measure* is restricted to exposing its own exclusion from the text.

Marcus, Leah, *Puzzling Shakespeare: Local Reading and its Discontents* (Berkeley and Los Angeles: University of California Press, 1988). Reads *Measure for Measure* in terms of anxieties affecting local and international politics in Jacobean London, as part of a larger argument in her book for attending to 'the deep cultural and political embeddedness' of literary texts.

Maus, Katherine Eisaman, *Inwardness and Theater in the English Renaissance* (Chicago: Chicago University Press, 1995). Investigates the play's fascination with sexual secrecy as part of an exploration of Renaissance preoccupations with religious, legal, and theatrical ways of understanding truth as inward and invisible.

Miles, Rosalind, *The Problem of 'Measure for Measure': A Historical Investigation* (London: Vision Press, 1976). Thorough and informative study that pairs a detailed survey of the play's reception history with a consideration of the theatrical conventions it uses.

Mullaney, Steven, *The Place of the Stage: License, Play and Power in Renaissance England* (Chicago: Chicago University Press, 1988). Investigates strategies of social and theatrical power deployed in *Measure for Measure* in the context of a lively and influential new historicist exploration of the cultural role of theatre in early modern London.

Nicholls, Graham, *'Measure for Measure': Text and Performance* (Basingstoke: Macmillan, 1986). Considers some issues raised by staging the play, by means of a brief account of its theatre history and detailed case studies of four modern productions.

Rossiter, A. P., *Angel with Horns and Other Shakespeare Lectures* (London: Longman, 1961). Defines problem plays as tragicomedies, and argues that the ambiguities of the play are embedded in its structure.

Rutter, Carol, *Clamorous Voices: Shakespeare's Women Today* (London: Women's Press, 1988). Includes an interesting chapter illustrating how some women who have played Isabella in recent Royal Shakespeare Company performances approached the role.

Skura, Meredith Anne, *The Literary Use of the Psychoanalytic Process* (New Haven, Conn.: Yale University Press, 1981). Sensitive presentation of some of the key concepts of psychoanalytic theory, arguing that the resources of psychoanalysis may be particularly helpful in interpreting a problematic play like *Measure for Measure*.

Stead, C. K. (ed.), *Shakespeare, 'Measure for Measure': A Casebook* (Basingstoke: Macmillan, 1971). Useful compendium of critical assessments.

Tillyard, E. M. W., *Shakespeare's Problem Plays* (London: Chatto & Windus, 1950). Argues that no single critical perspective can adequately deal with the various problems posed by the play.

Williamson, Marilyn L., *The Patriarchy of Shakespeare's Comedies* (Detroit, Mich.: Wayne State University Press, 1986). Argues that the play tests the limits of patriarchal power, particularly its attempts to regulate sexuality.

Wood, Nigel (ed.), *Measure for Measure* (Buckingham: Open University Press, 1996). Contains essays approaching the play from four distinct theoretical positions, in order both to generate new readings of *Measure for Measure* and to demonstrate the usefulness of these critical strategies.

Index

Pericles 49
plague 9, 48, 51
pleasure 19, 29–30, 38, 43, 51
politics 1–3; sexual, 48, 56
poverty 22, 29, 43, 51
power 2, 7, 8–13, 20, 22, 27,
  56–7, 58, 59, 66–7;
  theatrical 38, 39
prison 8, 11, 14–20, 25, 27, 32,
  40–1, 42, 46, 49, 51, 54, 56–
  7, 62, 64
prostitution 48–50, 52, 54
Protestantism 29
psychoanalysis 30–1, 35, 37
punishment 15–16, 18–20, 27,
  32, 43, 51, 65

religion 2, 4, 6, 7, 14, 28–9
revenge tragedy 66
ritual 20, 61
Romeo and Juliet 44, 55
Rose, Jacqueline 37
Royal Shakespeare Company
  1, 20, 33, 53, 61, 67

sexuality 1–3, 20–22, 32–3, 35–
  7, 39–40, 45, 49–51, 53–4,
  58–60
silence 20, 33, 39–41, 67–8
Singh, Jyotsna 51
Spanish Tragedy, The 66

stage 2, 9, 18, 20–1, 24–5, 48,
  54–5, 57, 61, 63
stage directions 8, 19, 25
Stevenson, Juliet, 33, 67–8
Stubbes, Philip 46–7
substitution 3, 5, 11, 36
surveillance 12–14, 59

theatre 4, 14, 16, 17, 20, 28,
  30, 32, 42, 44, 48, 51, 61, 63,
  67
Tempest, The 4, 10, 24
Titus Andronicus 66
torture 24, 37, 65
tragedy 24, 60–1, 66
tragicomedy 61
Troilus and Cressida 25, 58
Twelfth Night 25, 41
Two Noble Kinsmen, The 55

unconscious 30–1, 33-5, 37

Vienna 8–13, 15–16, 19–20,
  24–7, 29–30, 32, 37, 42–3,
  48, 52–3, 56–7, 62, 66

Wagner, Richard, 3
Whitney, Isabella 47–8
Wilson, Richard 13–14
Winter's Tale, The 25